MADAM FOREMAN

A RUSH TO JUDGMENT?

MADAM FOREMAN

A RUSH TO JUDGMENT?

BY

Armanda Cooley, Carrie Bess, and Marsha Rubin-Jackson

WITH A FORUM INCLUDING
**Willie Cravin, Tracy Hampton, Jeanette Harris,
Tracy Kennedy, and Michael Knox**

AS TOLD TO
TOM BYRNES

WITH

Mike Walker

DOVE
BOOKS

ISBN 0-7871-0918-5

Printed in the United States of America

Dove Books
301 North Cañon Drive
Beverly Hills, CA 90210

Distributed by Penguin USA

Text design and layout by Stanley S. Drate/Folio Graphics Co., Inc.
Jacket design and layout by Bear Canyon Creative
Jacket photograph by Jennifer Howard

First Printing: November 1995

10   9   8   7   6   5   4   3   2   1

Acknowledgments

This book would not have been possible without the superhuman effort of Jacqueline Melnick who worked around the clock and maintained her sense of humor throughout. Thanks also go to Mike Walker, Julie McCarron, and Lee Montgomery. Special thanks go to Mary Aarons and Michael Viner for giving me this opportunity.

—T.B.

Acknowledgments

I would like to thank God for giving me the opportunity to have served on the jury panel and I'd like to thank him for the opportunity to have met thirteen lovely people who will always be a part of my life. I would like to give a special thanks to my daughter whom I love so dearly, Yolanda Cooley. I would just like to say thank you for being there and supporting your mother during her time of need. I know that there were times in your own personal life when you had your own personal problems but you were always still there for me and I will never forget it as long as I live.

I would like to thank my brother, Gary Moore, who came to see his big sister every two weeks like clockwork. I know that there were several Sundays that your back was out and you were in tremendous pain but you still came right on. Thank you, brother.

I would like to thank my long term friend Sarah Coe and her family who took time out of busy days. During illnesses and other traumatic episodes, they still came to see about me and just to support me and to let me know that they were available if I ever needed anything.

Another special thanks to my friend, Helen Whitaker, who would bring her grandson in periodically just to cheer us up but especially for the time and the effort that you spent just running around and ordering things for us. Fixing us home cooked meals. These things were so greatly appreciated.

A big special thank you to my friend Carol Taylor. I have not known you, Carol, a lot of years. It just seems like a lifetime. I used to always tell you that fate had united our friendship together for some particular reason and maybe, just maybe, this was the reason. During my nine months of sequestration, you only missed approximately two Sundays of visiting. And I know it started off with all my family and friends just coming and visiting me but it ended up that everybody was coming to visit the family. I said that to say, Carol, the family thanks you for the running around you did for us, the purchasing of school clothes for the grandchildren, the home-cooked meals and a special thanks for the apple turnovers that are probably still lingering on some of our hips. We thank you and your kindness will always, always be remembered.

I'd like to thank my mother, Eva Comer, for her love and her long-distance moral support.

I would also like to thank my brothers, Howard and Louis Moore, and my sister, Greta Gillis, for their long-distance support and assistance in helping out my daughter, Yolanda, during her time of need.

—Armanda Cooley

We would like to dedicate this book to all the "extra-ceptional" people.

—ARMANDA COOLEY
—CARRIE BESS
—MARSHA RUBIN-JACKSON

For better or for worse, *The People vs. O.J. Simpson* served as a mirror of modern America. It was all there—wealth, fame, celebrity, sex, race, adultery, drugs, domestic abuse, and murder—acted out by a cast that cut across all segments of society in a drama that polarized the nation. And to witness it, all anyone had to do was turn on the television.

As winter turned to spring and spring to summer, opinions formed and then hardened. Research polls reported deep divisions along racial lines and the opinion pages filled with commentary that tried to explain how so many could look at the same evidence and reach such starkly different conclusions. But what people saw in the trial of the century simply reflected their own backgrounds and beliefs. In the end, that was the most revealing verdict of all.

Capturing the experiences of the jurors who decided this trial was not an easy feat. Throughout this book the insights and opinions of the primary narrators, Juror #230, foreperson Armanda Cooley; Juror #98, Carrie Bess; and Juror #984, Marsha Rubin-Jackson, are expressed in their own voices. Only they can reveal the view from the jury box.

—Tom Byrnes
Los Angeles, 1995

Contents

MADAM FOREMAN

A RUSH TO JUDGMENT?

1

FREE AT LAST

Los Angeles Superior Court Building
Judge Ito's Courtroom
Tuesday, October 3, 1995, 10:22 A.M.

JUDGE LANCE ITO: *And the record should reflect that we have now been rejoined by all the members of our jury panel and our alternates. Good morning again, ladies and gentlemen. All right, Mrs. Robertson, do you have the envelope with the sealed verdicts in those, please?*

MRS. ROBERTSON: *Yes, Your Honor.*

JUDGE LANCE ITO: *All right, would you give those to Deputy Trauer? And would you return those to our foreperson, juror number one? All right, Madam Foreperson, would you please open the envelope and check the condition of the verdict forms? All right, Madam Foreperson, you've had the opportunity to review the verdict forms?*

MADAM FOREPERSON: *Yes.*

JUDGE LANCE ITO: *Are they the same forms that you signed and are they in order?*

MADAM FOREPERSON: *Yes, they are.*

JUDGE LANCE ITO: *All right, would you hand those, please, to Deputy Trauer? And you have signed and dated those verdict forms, indicating the jury's verdict?*

MADAM FOREPERSON: *Yes.*

JUDGE LANCE ITO: *All right, thank you. All right, ladies and gentlemen, and the jury, I'm going to ask that you carefully listen to the verdicts as they are being read by the clerk, Mrs. Robertson, as after*

1

the verdicts have been read, you will be asked if these are your ver-
dicts, and I would caution the audience during the course of the read-
ing of these verdicts to remain calm, and if there is any disruption
during the reading of the verdicts, the bailiffs will have the obligation
to remove any persons disrupting these proceedings. All right, Mrs.
Robertson? All right, Mr. Simpson, would you please stand and face
the jury? Mrs. Robertson?

MRS. ROBERTSON: *Superior Court of California, County of Los* Angeles, *in the matter of the* People of the State of California vs. Oren-thal James Simpson, *we the jury, in the above entitled action, find the defendant, Orenthal James Simpson, not guilty of the crime of murder in violation of penal code section 187a, a felony, upon Nicole Brown Simpson, a human being, as charged in count one of the information. Superior Court of the State of California, County of Los Angeles, in the matter of the* People of the State of California vs. Orenthal James Simpson, *we the jury, in the above entitled action, find the defendant, Orenthal James Simpson, not guilty of the crime of murder, in viola-tion of penal code section 187a, a felony, upon Ronald Lyle Goldman, a human being, as charged in count two of the information. We the jury, in the above entitled action, further find the special circum-stance that the defendant, Orenthal James Simpson, has in this case been convicted of at least one crime of murder in the first degree and one or more crimes of murder of the first or second degree to be not true. Signed, this second day of October, 1995. Jury 230. Ladies and gentlemen of the jury, is this your verdict, say you one, say you all?*
JURY: *Yes.*

Ladies and gentlemen of the jury, is this your verdict, say you one, say you all?" Mrs. Robertson asked. I remember hearing my-self, Madam Foreman, Armanda Cooley, Juror #230, Seat 1, an-swer, "Yes," and I listened to the word echo across the courtroom, cutting through a swirl of sobs and smiles from the gallery of onlookers. After Deirdre Robertson read our verdict in the Peo-ple's case against O.J. Simpson, we the jury stood in the elevated box that had held us as prisoners of justice for 267 days. We were numb listening to the onslaught of sounds of grief and joy, our eyes darting around the courtroom, taking in the faces that had stared at us over the long months of trial for one last time. I don't think I'll forget those faces, always searching our every expression, our every gesture, our every sign of body language for a tip-off as to what we were thinking throughout the trial. But that day, the last day, all sounds and shapes seemed to run together into a jumble of faces in the courtroom.

While we were standing there, I saw friend and fellow juror #98, Carrie Bess, look hopelessly into the crowd. "I will never forget that moment," Carrie said later. "The look on the faces. The first thing I heard, coming from my left side, was the outcry of the Goldmans. I heard Ron Goldman's sister, Kim, yell out in pain. I turned to look and saw the face of Ron's stepmother. I saw her tenseness. And you could feel it. Across the courtroom I saw O.J. and Johnnie Cochran, Jr. They had their hands clutched. Cochran laid his head on O.J.'s shoulder. Oh, the pain. Deep down inside me, with all the crying and moaning, I could feel it. It was choking me. The tension was terrible. Tears were flowing down faces. I could feel myself about to erupt. I started to cry myself."

I don't think any of us can sort out those final moments, but I remember O.J. Simpson catching my eye as he waved at us, mouthing, "Thank you," smiling in that dazed, delighted way that children do when they're told they're getting off without a spanking. *My God,* I thought. *We're all in shock.*

Everybody was looking at everybody. All the players in the drama that had gripped America seemed stunned that the last act had ended. I watched my co-jurors as they looked about the courtroom in disbelief. Our ordeal was finally over and our minds began to toy with the thought of a long-awaited homecoming. All around us were the supporting cast—bailiffs, clerks, court reporters, and journalists such as Dominick Dunne of *Vanity Fair,* Jeffrey Toobin of *The New Yorker,* and the reporters we had dubbed Broke-Neck and Blinky. The superstars—a jubilant Johnnie Cochran and his back-slapping defense team—milled about as a devastated Chris Darden stared at us, strangely serene, and Marcia Clark began reaching out to comfort her colleagues. And above all the gasps of surprise could be heard the eerie cries and agonized sobs from the Goldman family.

Sitting high above the theater he had ruled for months on end, Judge Ito, the director of this drama that had so often lapsed into black comedy and outright farce, paused reflectively, recounting the list of procedures to be completed before bringing the trial to an end. And then, with the authority vested in him by the state of California, he dismissed his court.

I felt my heart leap in my chest and come to rest somewhere below my throat. *Free at last*, I thought. *We're going home!* But then I caught myself. Not home; not at first. No, myself and jurors #984 and #98, Marsha Rubin-Jackson and Carrie Bess, had some final business to attend to before we would be able to sit in our own living rooms or sleep between our own sheets. Together, we had made plans in order to avoid the media onslaught we knew was coming and take a few days to decompress. My daughter Yolanda would be waiting at the secret drop-off point where the families had been instructed to come to pick up the jurors. I had no idea where that drop-off point was, but I could hardly wait to get there.

The group filed out of the box and made a final trip back to the jury room, where no one bothered to take a seat. Instead, we stood, wiping the odd tear away and letting some of the emotions we had held back so long seep out. A moment later, Judge Ito bustled into the room and politely thanked everyone, made a few passing jokes, said he hoped to see us all again sometime, and left. Then the door opened and a team of court-appointed psychologists walked in. I looked at the others, especially Marsha, because she seemed the most surprised.

"The psychologists started telling us what we were going to feel," recalls Marsha. "Looking back, it was all accurate and very useful information. But at that precise moment, all I could think about was going home. It was making me mad to hear these psychologists talk to me right then. We'd been lied to and conned for months about when we'd be released from our incarceration. Now I'd handed in my decision and I wanted to be taken to that pickup point to meet my family. I wasn't going directly home, but I wanted my freedom. Funny thing, now that I look back on all that has happened, at that moment I hadn't even considered what anyone else would think of the verdict we'd passed on O.J. Simpson. I don't think any of us knew what was coming."

The psychologists stayed forty-five minutes, trying to help us all focus on what we might encounter in the coming days. Then, sensing that not keeping us weary jurors a moment longer than necessary was the surest way to ward off possible future depression, they ended their comments and asked for questions. There were none. There was a moment's pause. Capturing the mood, someone muttered, "Now can we *please* get out of here?"

Sergeant Steve Smith, a man everyone had come to regard as a close friend—we even called him "Pops"—swung the door open and said, "Let's go, folks!" I fell in behind him and the other jurors followed. Together we filed down the eleventh-floor corridor and got into the elevator for the last time. After months of being herded in and out of the courthouse, we all had become very familiar with the elevator banks and corridors, but everyone was surprised when the elevator stopped at the tenth floor. None of us had been there before, but we knew it was called "the Lockup," an ominous place where defendants and jailhouse witnesses needed for trials were held until called for their moment in court. As we stepped out of the car, a strange chill descended on the group. The floor was lined with cells that had square-peephole doors and clipboards on which prisoner information was tracked. Standing in front of the cells was a long line of uniformed deputies, none of whom seemed either friendly or familiar.

In all of our months of trudging through the back stairs and hallways of the courthouse, we the "O.J. Jurors" had become the

equivalent of "regulars." Recognized and accepted by the courthouse workers and law enforcement officers who nodded or hailed
us with a smile as we passed, suddenly we found ourselves amid
strangers. The deputies stared flatly, silently, betraying no emotion. Carrie told me she felt her insides churn at the fearful sensa-
tion that descended over the group. "They're all white," she
whispered. Walking behind Pops, I knew that the thick, vaguely
menacing atmosphere wasn't my or Carrie's imagination working
overtime. *My God, they hate us for our verdict,* I thought. Then,
in bewilderment, *How could they? It's not fair.*

I could sense Marsha scooting right up behind me. She told
me later that all of a sudden she didn't feel safe. "I wanted to be
near a friend," Marsha explains. "I kept thinking, *What the hell is
this? Why are they acting like this?*"

I looked beyond the icy display in the hallway, quietly wondering, *Is it just these deputies? Or does everyone hate our verdict?*
But Carrie was the first to break the eerie silence. "Oh my God
. . . Hell. I'm sort of afraid," she said, looking around. "I feel that
they're angry at us." Another juror spoke, "If they're upset with
us because of the verdict . . ." Carrie rejoined, "They shouldn't
be." In a show of bravado, a female juror said, "Oh, come on, Bess,
we won't worry about that. We'll just keep moving."

As she walked through this strange place, Carrie remembers
looking back to the moment before the verdict was announced
and feeling the chill run deeper. "I kept glancing around the
courtroom before the verdict was read. I was very nervous because
I knew what it was, and I didn't know how the world was going to
take it. Then the judge opened the verdict, read it, then passed it
to the clerk to be read aloud. And I was thinking about when the
judge dismissed us, how all of us cried, even the men, although
they tried to hold it back. As we filed back into the jury room, we
hugged each other. We were saying our good-byes, saying how
much we'd miss each other. Then they took us out, took us that

way we'd never been before, through this place they called 'the Lockup.'

"It was the first time I'd been through there," recalls Carrie. "It was one of the most chilling things you ever felt in your life. It was like running a gauntlet. I felt I'd committed a crime and I was on my way to being locked up. As we passed the deputies they would look at us and the feeling that you got was . . . terrible, so cold. I can't explain it. I was frightened, tense. I wondered if the rest of the world felt like we'd done wrong."

I kept my eyes straight ahead as we stayed close to Sergeant Steve Smith. *Thank God Sergeant Smith is here,* I thought.

Finally we came to an elevator we'd never used before, one reserved for the transport of prisoners. The walls nearby were a mural of scrawled graffiti: names, dates, times, and messages from the men and women who shuttled through the justice system every day. There was a wait for the elevator, perhaps a couple of minutes, but it seemed like an eternity to me. Sensing our tension, Sergeant Smith asked a deputy from the Lockup what was taking so long. "This elevator isn't like the ones you've been riding. You have to be patient," came the reply.

What a strange thing to say, I thought. Maybe it was paranoia. Hell, I don't know. I don't know what I was feeling. I still had mixed emotions. I was glad to get out of there but I still didn't know what I had to face once I got out of there, and now there was all this cloak-and-dagger stuff. That was why we'd been walking through the Lockup in the first place. It was a plan to get us out of the courthouse to the drop-off point without the media or anybody else bothering us. I don't think most people know this, but there were three or four bomb threats every week during nearly the entire period of sequestration. If some nut wanted to nail the entire O.J. jury, this would be their last opportunity. So when we finally caught that elevator and got off in the underground parking area under the courthouse, things really got scary.

As part of the high-security plan devised by the Los Angeles

Sheriff's Department, the usual vans that transported us to and from the courthouse had been replaced by a full-size black-and-white bus with barred windows. As we exited the elevator, we were hustled to a cordon of armed guards and onto the bus. After we took our seats, one of the officers issued commands: "People, it's very important that you keep your heads down below the level of the bus windows as we exit the underground area. No one knows that the jury is aboard this bus and that's how we'd like to keep it. We need your cooperation. It will be some time before we reach the drop-off point where your families will be waiting. But when I give you the signal, please put your head down, repeat, down below the level of the windows until we reach our destination. . . . Okay, driver, we're all in place. Everybody, please put your heads down NOW! Okay, driver. Head out."

I and a few others couldn't resist peeking timidly under the bottom of the bus windows as we roared up out of the underground garage and into the sunlight. I turned and looked at Carrie and Marsha. They, too, were peeking.

"It was shocking," says Carrie. "When we came up from out of the underground there were policemen as far as you could see. Cops on horseback, cops in riot gear . . . I've never seen so many police in my life. I'm not talking thirty or forty. I'm talking what looked like hundreds of law enforcement officers. That was scary in itself. I thought, *Why do they need so many policemen? Do they really think we're going to be assassinated? It would take a small army to break through this crowd.* But once we got through the crowd of cops, I expected we'd be part of a big caravan. But the only vehicle that was there, I believe, was Sergeant Smith in an unmarked car leading the bus. There might have been one car behind the bus, but that was all. As we sort of sneaked peeks under the bottom of our windows, it didn't look like anybody had spotted us . . . No media, or anything like that. But then one of the jurors shouted, 'Hey, we got helicopters overhead.' But one of the deputies on the bus just smiled and told us, 'Don't worry about it, they're police helicopters.' "

We were relieved. The plan worked perfectly. No one followed us to our secret destination—the Sheriff's Academy in Whittier, California, not too far from Downtown L.A. Fifteen minutes after we had pulled out from under the courthouse, the bus rolled into the gated compound. Looking out the windows, we could see armed deputies everywhere as we drove through another gate that opened and closed behind us. Deputies quickly surrounded the bus as we were told, "Okay, we're here."

"This was a place that used to house prisoners, but they don't use it for that anymore," Marsha explains. "It's a training facility with a lot of classrooms and meeting rooms. As we got off the bus, we were led into a large room. I don't know who could have gotten in there to do us harm, but we were still surrounded by deputies. They told us, 'We'll wait here until your families come and pick you up.' After a while, families started arriving. Before long, it seemed like everyone in that room was crying. All the jurors started saying good-bye to each other, knowing that this might be the last time that we'd ever meet. Everyone was exchanging phone numbers. I remember saying to Armanda that it was finally Freedom Day for the 'Mole People.' That was one of our names for ourselves because we were always stuck away from the light and hidden. We also used to call ourselves the 'Groundhogs' because we were always brought into a building from the underground and left the same way."

Then a peculiar thing happened. In a room next door to where the jurors were meeting their families, a deputy had turned on a TV set. One of the officers who had guarded the jurors during sequestration stared at the screen idly. "Hey, everybody, come here," he suddenly called out, "and tell Armanda her daughter is on TV." I followed everybody as they rushed into the TV room. Then habit set in. We started eyeing each other uncertainly, worry etched on everyone's face. "We were all looking at each other and wondering if it was okay to actually watch TV," says Marsha. "We'd been forbidden to see anything but video movies for so long. It was incredible. We still felt like prisoners."

But then, as we watched TV for the first time since the trial began, we learned what was really happening. We were being judged in a forum far tougher than anything the legal system would permit: the world of public opinion. After being secluded from the real world, the shock of sudden re-entry sank in. Bathed in the screen's blue light, we stood silent save for the occasional gasp as we watched the hordes of so-called O.J. experts—most of them completely unknown to most of us—trash our verdict as "racist" and "hasty" and "ill-conceived."

"It just tore me down," remembers Carrie. "I watched Gil Garcetti and a lot of big-time attorneys criticizing us, talking about how it was such a speedy decision. They weren't there. If they were in my shoes, they'd have done the same thing. The nerve of them. How could they say it's a racial thing? Don't open up that wound with us. Don't drop that ball on us. Race was here before we went in that room. It will be here after we're buried and gone."

Standing in the center of the group, I quietly shook my head. So many feelings were darting around, but as bad as it seemed that moment, the worst was yet to come.

2

HOMEWARD BOUND

We're sitting in that hotel room feeling that O.J. is free.
He's home with his family. He's laughing.
He's having a good time and enjoying the moment,
whatever it was,
of freedom and here we are fugitives from justice . . .
We're running, trying to hide from the media . . .
—ARMANDA COOLEY

When all our friends and relatives drove out to the pickup point at the Sheriff's Academy in Whittier, they had to show ID to get in. Marsha and I had already planned to go to Las Vegas instead of going home right away. Carrie was going to Vegas, too, just a day later—she wanted to go home to see her house first. The three of us had been through a lot and we just wanted to give ourselves a couple of days to relax. Besides, Carrie's a gambler.

I had arranged for my girlfriend Carol to pick up Marsha and me. She had already made our travel plans. Before she left to get us, she made sure that there was nobody around her house since we already knew that the media were everywhere and that our places had been staked out. We had decided that if they were around her house, we would go up to her mom's house before we went to the airport. Luckily, there was nobody at Carol's. Once we arrived, we called Marsha's mother because she was also going with us, and we wanted to let her know where she should be dropped off.

This sounds complicated, but we wanted to make sure Carol was not followed. Marsha's niece Jordan Hine had been followed by a reporter when she went to the bank the day before. Meanwhile, my daughter Yolanda was also planning on going with us but she couldn't get out of the house because the street was flooded with media people. So we agreed to meet on the plane. She called the Los Angeles Police Department and they came out and escorted her to the airport. That's how insane it was.

Before we were released, the sheriffs told us that if we had any problems, we should call the L.A.P.D. They were on alert and would provide any assistance we or our families needed. When I heard this, I'm thinking to myself, *Hell, we got to call the L.A.P.D.? Like they're going to help us now?* But Yolanda did call and they did help her out of there. They even followed her in a helicopter to make sure no one else was following the car.

So that was the plan: Marsha, Carrie, my daughter Yolanda, Marsha's mother, and me were all going to Vegas. My daughter knew the pit boss at Bally's. On one of our visits during the trial, I had told her that when this thing was over, I wanted to go to either San Francisco or Vegas and lay up for a couple of days just to find my bearings. She said, "Well, Mom, let me call my friend Chris out in Vegas and see what he can do. Maybe they'll give you some kind of deal." So she called him up and he said they would comp the room for us as long as it wasn't the week of November fourth—I guess they were having some big fight or something right around then. So that's how that came about. I guess they probably figured they would be on TV and we would give them a little advertising or something, but it never worked out that way.

After all the madness of being released from the courthouse and the warnings about the media crush, it was a real relief just being in Vegas, in a place where no one was looking for you like they were back in L.A. And the fact that you knew someone was looking for you, hunting you, was what made you uncomfortable. I always felt that if it wasn't for the media attention, no one would have recognized us anyway. After all, we weren't recognized even when we went out on outings during the trial. Well, a couple times people recognized us because the deputies were with us— some of them had been seen on TV a lot, so they were recognized—and that gave away who we were. We used to tell them all the time, "Hell, you all can leave and let us go. You guys stay here because you're the ones causing trouble."

On the plane to Vegas, Yolanda and Marsha's mother told us about what was going on in the media. It was a frightening situation. You felt scared. And it's not like you're in a position where you can just pick up and move to get away from it. Not everyone can afford to just pick up and find another place to live. And I guess that's probably what excited us about listening to all these money charms that we started hearing about—the kind of money people were talking about if we did a story with them. You think you can use that cash and you can pick up and move, that it will save you from having to deal with all these different things. But at that time, we really did not know what we were going to do. I don't think anybody on the jury did. The only thing we wanted to do is just get home and try to get back to reality. That was the main thing. As a matter of fact, Carrie did manage to get home that night. She sneaked in late. "I just had to see it," she told me. "Just had to, because when I first got out, my daughter took me to her apartment. Then, after just being there a few minutes, here comes the *L.A. Times* man. My son came over to see me and I told him to keep an eye on my house and that when it got quiet there and the media left—I didn't care if it's one or two o'clock at night—call me and let me slip in.

"Well, what happened was about ten o'clock there was only one car on the street. My tenant in the front house called my son and told him there was just one car out front and that if I wanted to come home, this was probably the best time. So my daughter drove me over to the neighborhood and parked in the driveway. My tenant opened her front door to distract anyone who might have been out there, and I went in through her back door and entered my apartment that way as opposed to going through the side, like I normally would. As I jumped out of the car and ran into the tenant's house, the lady sitting in the car out front jumped out and yelled, 'Hey, are you Carrie Bess?' And I just ran on in and didn't say anything. They had all the lights out so no one could see, and I stood there in the dark. Then my daughter brought my luggage in.

"The reporter stayed outside for a while. I heard my dog barking at her. Finally, she went to my next-door neighbor's house and gave him a card to give me. I still don't know who it was because I gave the card to the tenant downstairs. I wasn't going to talk to anyone, and besides, I was busy trying to get into my room. When I walked in my bedroom, I literally almost passed out. I had been sending all my clothes home once it looked like we were getting into closing arguments, and it was like the kids just dumped them out wherever they could and brought the luggage back. I had about fifteen bags full of clothes and things. The bed was full. The walls were full. It was just clothes, clothes, and more clothes everywhere I looked. I almost panicked. So I worked until about two-thirty that morning just cleaning up.

"When I finally got to bed, I couldn't sleep. I just lay there twitching. I was so jumpy knowing I had to get up at four A.M. to go to the airport. So I never went to sleep. I literally got up, took a shower, grabbed my things, and my son took me to the airport, where I met my girlfriend Sheila. We were on a five-thirty A.M. flight because we got that two-for-one deal. I had tried to go with Armanda and Marsha after we were all released, but they already had their flight booked and I couldn't get a reservation. Well, I could, but they wanted $144 for one person and I wouldn't pay it.

So Sheila flew with me the next day on a 'friends-fly-free' special that was offered on flights at off hours.

"It was strange," Carrie continues. "Everybody on the airplane was reading newspapers and all of the papers were about the verdict. Everybody had a comment. Sheila kept whispering all these things to me. I said, 'Shut up. Don't say "you guys." Don't whisper to me. I'm nervous.' She wanted to talk about it, but I didn't want to, especially not then and there. After she hears them, she says, 'Boy, you would be up the creek right now if they really knew who you were.' And I looked at her and said, 'Shut up,' because we were in the air, and I'm trapped, and what's going to stop them if they know who I am?"

"I know what you mean about Sheila. It was exciting to my mother, too," says Marsha. "Right before being released, I kept saying, 'Don't tell anyone that I am going to Vegas. I don't want anyone knowing.' I don't know if I had foreseen what was going to take place after it was over. I just had in my mind that I didn't want to talk about it, at least until I was ready to talk about it. But it was just like the excitement of it for her. She couldn't understand. 'What's the big deal? You're doing your duty.' And I'm going, 'Well, when I get out of here, I just want to go home. I don't want the phone ringing. I don't want to talk about that.'"

I agreed. When we were on the plane that night, listening to people talking about it, you're just sort of scooting down in your seat, trying to be inconspicuous. You're thinking that they would recognize you, like you had this big sign on you saying "Armanda Cooley: O.J. juror. I'm the one. I'm the one who passed the verdict to Judge Ito." You just slid down in the seat. You wanted to read the newspaper, but you're sort of nervous about it and can't really focus. And my daughter Yolanda, well, she was sort of nervous, too, because she got caught up in the media frenzy. See, they got to her while we were at the Sheriff's Academy waiting to be picked up. She was on TV saying that she was glad it was over and that all she wanted was for her mom to come home and how she just wanted to kiss me. Still, she was the one who got us out of there and off to Vegas. We had told her as soon as the verdict comes down, call the airlines and get us some tickets.

When we got to Vegas, we checked in and just took it easy. That was Tuesday night, October third. Carrie arrived the next day. We ate, gambled a bit, lost money, walked around, just took it easy, and did what we wanted because that's exactly what we couldn't do during sequestration. We were always told when and where to be and rarely had the chance to go outside, so we just enjoyed the time together. After Carrie arrived the three of us sat down to try and figure out what to do about the media. As much as we wanted to ignore it, we all had begun to realize that there was no escape.

Despite all the precautions we had taken, it didn't take the media long to track us down in Vegas. Dominick Dunne from *Vanity Fair* was the first. Evidently, he received a telephone call from the British tabloids. He got some information and then went on the evening news in Los Angeles and indicated that my daughter was on the phone making deals with companies before we even sat down to deliberate the verdict. I knew my daughter would never have done such a thing and she kept saying, "Mom, that is not true. Where's he getting this information from?" Besides, no one had called the house until after the deliberations had begun and there was no way you could negotiate a deal unless you did it personally. And who in the hell would call the British tabloids? We don't know any of them. If we had called anyone it would have been one of the tabloids in the United States.

It never dawned on us that Dunne was talking to one of the British tabloids. I believe it was *News of the World*, because that was the only one that knew where we were. They were pissed off because we declined to do a story with them until we had secured an attorney to negotiate for us. So they leaked the information that we had at least talked to them, I guess, and they also leaked the information that we were in Vegas. But all the other information they leaked was wrong. I heard it said that there were three or four of us in Vegas getting lines of credit at Bally's. Lines of credit? I don't know where Dunne got that from but the fact that he knew we were at Bally's leads me to believe that *News of the World* had to have given him that information.

"Well, what we did right after I arrived was sit down and discuss who had contacted us," Carrie adds. "Those were the papers that we went over. What were their offers? Then we saw that Brenda [Moran] was on the media. That was the next thing we discussed. Then we talked about the fact that Yolanda knew someone she was supposed to contact if we wanted to sell our story. It was someone who had contacted her at home in an attempt to get to us after we were released. She told them she wasn't going to do anything until we decided what we wanted to do.

"So we talked a bit and then went and ate. Then we gambled a little bit and Marsha, her mother, and Armanda went for a little tour. I think they were going to show Marsha's mother the new casinos and things on the strip, but I wanted to keep on gambling," Carrie continues. "Of course, I was tied to one machine, as usual. When I go to Vegas, I usually sit in one area. Then they came back and got me and said, 'Well, we have to talk some business.' At that point, we were just running away. We didn't even think about it—selling our story or how we were going to deal with the media. As a matter of fact, we hadn't even thought of anything like that. We were just going to get away. I was flying to Vegas and I was going to be there for two days and then I had set up a flight for me to go back East on Saturday. I was going to see my family for two or three weeks, and my daughter even took off school to go home with me."

"And my husband was expecting me in Hawaii that Thursday or Friday," Marsha says. "None of us were planning on dealing with the media. We just wanted to take a break together and then go home to our families and get away from it all."

People were trying to get at us from all over and were leaving messages everywhere. Yolanda had been taking the telephone calls and returning them for us. She listened to them all and in Vegas she told us, "Well, Mom, if you guys are going to do anything in the media, the whole key is an exclusive. You have to be more or less the first ones out there." I kept saying, "I don't want to hear that. I'll deal with that kind of stuff later. I do not want to deal with it right now." She kept saying, "Well, you guys need to think about dealing with it." At this time, I think, is when we heard Brenda was on TV.

"It seemed like she was on that TV all night long," Marsha remembers. "And it's not what she said so much as what she projected. Watching her seemed like our worst nightmare. She just seemed to be saying, 'Aw, screw that,' to a lot of the questions she was asked about the verdict being a miscarriage of justice. She didn't say that, but that's what she projected."

And that's what people saw and that's what they think she said. That comes about by not allowing yourself time to think before you speak. I mean, here you are: You've been in a situation, locked down, tied up for eight, nine months, and you're not allowed to even discuss the case. You're not allowed to discuss anything. And then there's this reaction and all of your feelings come out before you've even had a chance to deal with them.

And that was the reason why we did not want to get on TV. Because once you expose yourself on the TV, people know who you look like and you've got these crazy people out there. I said that and, at first, I was just talking. Right after the verdict my daughter was on TV for five seconds saying that she'll be glad when her mom comes home and how happy she was that it was over with. One day, after we came back from Vegas, she went shopping and some guy chased her down the street. "Well, how's your mom? Is your mom home yet? Aren't you the girl that was on TV?" She replied, "I'm afraid you're mistaken." After that happened she told me, "Mom, I'm glad you guys didn't get on the TV." She was gung-ho about us setting the record straight, especially after Brenda got on there. The reporters were all saying that they wanted us to get out and set the record straight. But I didn't think it was necessary.

"Yolanda was right about the exclusive," says Marsha. "My sister, Linda, was on the phone telling us the same thing. I guess it's from them asking her for an exclusive. She explained to me, 'Well, Marsha, this is what they want. An exclusive. And basically, the longer you guys sit, the better off you'll be.' But right then I had no intentions of talking to anybody."

It was crazy. We're sitting in that hotel room feeling that O.J. is free. He's home with his family. He's laughing. He's having a good time and enjoying the moment, whatever it was, of freedom and here we are fugitives from justice or of justice. We're running, trying to hide from the media, trying to get our lives together. The three of us still didn't know which direction to take or what we were going to do.

We didn't have any representation at this point. My daughter had been contacted by some man named Stewart from *News of the World* and he wanted to do a deal quickly. But Yolanda had a friend named Ron who was good friends with a man named Steven Lerman, who was an attorney, and she suggested that we get in touch with him, that he could help us sort through the offers that were starting to pour in.

While we were in Vegas, one British tabloid had offered me $250,000 and the other jurors $100,000 each for our stories. And I almost took the bait. But before I made a decision, Yolanda said, "Well, Mom, maybe we need to call Steve just so that once you make a decision to go with someone he can review the contract."

We called Steve in Los Angeles and he said, "Look, I don't have any experience in this thing that you guys are involved in. I'm going to be honest. But I do have experience with the media because of my role in the Rodney King case, and that's where I got the majority of my experience in how to deal with these people. And that's why I can be of help."

We had no idea what he was talking about at the time, but now I see what he meant. And the fact that he was honest, to tell us that he didn't know anything about this type of work but that he'd do his best, well, we appreciated that. So we agreed to work with him. He told us to sit tight and to let him call the tabloids first before any arrangements were made.

So Steve called some of the tabloids, talked to them, and of course they made no offer to him over the telephone. All of a sudden we had an attorney and things started to change. The real world started facing us at this time. Then Steve calls back and says, "Armanda, all they want is to drill you for a couple days and a couple nights. And what they do is they give you a Letter of Intent. And they take that information back to London and they try to find a buyer. If they cannot find a buyer, they'll tell you that they're sorry. They can't use the information. Here's a couple of thousand for your trouble." This was news to me.

But by this time, we were totally exposed. People are making all sorts of promises but you don't know what the hell they're printing in London. You're not there. You don't have any foreign correspondents who can tell you how your story is being told. When I heard how it worked, I was livid. While all this was going on, Marsha's sister was negotiating with these people in Los Angeles and everyone was flashing all these dollars at us. She received a call from the *Globe* and they offered us $200,000 for the story and $100,000 for book rights. It seemed like there was money in the air and we were truly getting excited. We're all poor little helpless black women, uneducated, ignorant, and, naturally, what we need is money. So, you're thinking a quarter of a million dollars and the immediate reaction is "Oh, yeah, I'll take it."

"That's right. My sister was back in California and we were calling her and we kept hearing that she was getting offers from the *Globe* and it kept getting higher with each call," Marsha says. "The girl's name was Charlene or something and she kept upping the ante each time they talked. So we would call, and my sister would call us back with a figure that would get higher and higher. It got up to $300,000 at one point. It was too much to handle and so we decided to turn her over to Steve."

We felt we were getting the runaround. We hadn't told anyone where we were, but the woman from the *Globe* told Marsha's sister that she was even willing to come to wherever we were at the moment. And we asked, "Okay, if she comes down, is she going to bring us a check?" Because we all agreed that they have to bring us the check. They can't come talking about a Letter of Intent. You know, I want the $200,000. I'll take the Letter of Intent on the book rights that will come later, but I want the cash up front. And we're hearing "Oh yes, we're bringing a cashier's check," and all this kind of stuff. It sounded good, but we wanted to check with Steve first.

So you can imagine how we felt when we had Steve call the person from the *Globe* and no money was offered. None whatsoever. All he heard was, "Well, no, I'm not in a position to make any type of offer." So, Steve says, "Well, I'll tell you what. We'll just make an appointment and I'll be happy to meet with you and your bosses in a couple of days and I'll have my clients come down."

It was just more of the same—claims that were completely out there, that had no basis in reality. Steve said, "It's so good that you guys didn't tell her where you were, because they would have been in Vegas like bats out of hell." So, he set up a meeting and told the three of us to return to L.A. early Thursday morning to meet with them and see what kind of deal would be offered. We were so nervous that I don't think any of us slept at all. We left Vegas early and Steve arranged for a limo to pick us up at the airport and take us to rooms he had reserved for us at the Beverly Prescott Hotel. He knew they would be watching our homes.

Originally our plan was to go to his office from the airport, but we got a call from his people, who told us not to come over, to wait, because by then NBC, CBS, and "Hard Copy" were all in the hallway outside his office. Later, Steve told us that he had stepped off the elevator only to have all these mikes in his face and the media looking for us.

When he met with the *Globe* without us, Steve brought up the offer we received while in Vegas—the $300,000—and the president of the *Globe* says, "Of course not. We can't offer them that type of money." His position was that Brenda had spoken already—for free. "What can your clients tell us that has not already been told? They missed the big money," he said. "They should have been here Tuesday, but they were so busy running, they missed the big money." Steve kept asking, "What is the big money? What kind of money are you talking about?" I think that he eventually said something about $40,000 for the foreman and $20,000 for the other jurors, but that never did come out in a formal offer.

And none of us approved of that, of the way these people did business. I feel that if you have somebody out there representing your company and they're making offers your company does not support, then your credibility is torn down as far as I'm concerned. I understand there are freelancers out there, but then I also understand they're just looking for a lot of dirt. I felt that dirt is not really what we had. We're talking about our lives and how our lives had been disrupted for nine months.

"Besides, we had also learned that the *Globe* had published photos of the victims, Ron and Nicole, and none of us approved of that," Marsha says.

Steve suggested it might be a good idea if we did a book. He wanted us to make up our own minds, but he told us this really wasn't a tabloid story. He said he was familiar with Michael Viner of Dove Books. He said Dove was a good company and that writing a book was probably the best way to handle it. That way, we would get money up front and then have money coming in consistently as the book sells. But it was also a way of making sure that we got the story out as honestly as possible. Because after these tabloids get through with you, you don't know what the hell's going on.

And that's the reason why we decided to do a book. After we thought about it, the *Globe,* the *Star,* and all those tabloids . . . I'm not going to compromise myself for that kind of garbage and let them put a picture of me on a horse's body and say, "This is the foreperson and this is what she looked like" and take what we said and print it all out of context. These are important issues, and they need to be reported as honestly as we can remember them.

We thought it over and decided to talk with Dove over the next few days. We stayed on at the Beverly Prescott Hotel and laid low. We all had dinner in Carrie's room that night and made some phone calls.

"I had already called my husband from Las Vegas because I was supposed to go meet him that Thursday," Marsha remembers. "I was supposed to fly to Hawaii. I had called him on Wednesday night and told him to come to Los Angeles, that I couldn't handle it, that there was no way I could get out at this time. So he flew into Los Angeles that Thursday night, and then Friday morning he and my mother went to check on the house to see what was going on over there. Then he came back down that Friday evening and we stayed at the hotel until Saturday. We stayed together until Carrie left on Saturday morning and went back to Vegas."

"But before I left, we used the time to get to know Steve better," adds Carrie. "We sipped a little wine and chatted and had group sessions and talked and got to know him. We were also starting to read the papers and watch a little TV and get Steve's perspective on what had been going on."

"That was interesting because the whole time I was in Vegas I didn't even hear people there say anything about the case," Marsha says. "Well, once a man called to me over the table and asked me what I thought about the verdict, in a general way, nothing specific. But other than that, not one comment."

And that's when what we started to see in the media really caught us off guard. On the news you're hearing that 60 percent of the people are saying this was a verdict based on racism. You also hear the president of the United States saying that the country has been split as far as race is concerned because of this verdict. They pretend like racism never existed in this country, that throughout the years we managed to get rid of it and then, all of a sudden, based on our verdict in the jury, we brought it back. But I beg to differ with everybody. Racism has been a part of this country since I've been a part of this country and it has never, ever left. I can only hope and pray that eventually it will leave at one time or another. But everybody is using racism as a means of coming out of the closet and letting people know how they really feel. We the jury are not responsible for things that have been going on in this country for years.

Hearing all this put me in shock. I felt as if I had stepped into the Twilight Zone with all the media talking as if we were responsible for a problem that was hundreds of years old. Racism has permeated this country since Columbus's so-called discovery of America when it was already settled by Indians. It started right then and there. I feel that you had to have been in that jury box to know exactly what we were going through, and it wasn't based on race or anything like that. I think that a lot of the politicians—black and white—are using us to fight their political wars. They are using this case. I don't know what the heck they would have used if we had still been deliberating when election time would have come along, but it's just giving them some new ideas to use.

And it's not fair to us at all. Our whole lifestyle has changed. You can't go home to what used to be home. As far as TV programs or things like that, I haven't even been watching them because I'm feeling so hostile and so upset that I decided, "Wait a minute, Armanda, just calm yourself down. You can always come back to this stuff a little later. It's not even necessary for you to even watch this stuff because you feel the necessity to get out there and set the record straight." Then I realized a lot of people are just looking for somebody to badger and I just figured I'm not going to be the one. Not right now. Maybe later, after I've been able to relocate my life. But I don't think I'll ever be able to relocate my life. I think the media decided this case early on. I also think the fact that a lot of people out there judged Mr. Simpson guilty from the jump street is a violation of the law. The law states you are innocent until proven guilty. They needed to see someone punished from jump street. They had these preconceived ideas and it's not fair. The court never asked us if we personally thought the man was guilty of murder or not. The court provided us a law we had to go by and that's it. Our conclusion was based on that law.

Before this, we had never heard anything about the racial stuff. Remember, we were sequestered. I guess that's the reason why everybody on the jury was shocked at the way our decision was being interpreted. That racism was so heavily invoked, that racism was so heavily involved in the conversation and the people's reaction. Not surprised about racism itself, because, like I said, it's here and it's been here for ages, but about the fact that this trial was used to emphasize it even more. And accusing us of being racists. That's what's appalling to me.

It made us angry. As a matter of fact, Carrie Bess was so angry, she was about to make a decision to go on one of the TV programs just to set the record straight. We talked her out of it based on what Steve said to us. It's not that we were in hiding or anything, but the timing was just not right. I mean it's not that you need time to make up excuses, but you need time to think about who the hell you are, what you are, and what's happening to you. And you don't need anybody invading your privacy while you're going through all of that. When you've been locked up for eight or nine months, you have no privacy. If you went on TV you would have people invading your privacy at that particular time. Here's your moment alone in the world—a moment when you need to be alone or just with family—and you look out there and the whole world is against you. I mean, that's a scary feeling. It's almost like you want to go back to sequestration on the fifth floor at the Inter-Continental and try to find refuge some place.

As a result, we're still hiding from the fact that we were O.J. jurors. Let me give you an example. You know what happens when you're accustomed to going to the same places and you get to know the people who work there. I was at the cleaners one day after the trial was over and the girl at the counter asked me where I had been. Whenever this happens I usually say, "Well, I've just been hanging out." But for the first time I told her I had been on the jury, and I got such a weird feeling. I don't know if it was just embarrassment or relief. I mean, she wasn't derogatory about it. She just said, "Wow."

"I know what you mean, because I called a lady that I know in Miami and I happened to tell her," Carrie says. "She said, 'Well, what have you been up to?' I said, 'Whether you know it or not, I was on the Simpson case.' She said, 'My sister did tell me that you were on that case.' I said, 'Well, I'm out and I'm just taking care of some business.' Once you say it, it's like, what are the repercussions? What is going to happen? What are they going to say? Because when I first left for Vegas, I can remember people on that plane sitting and reading the newspaper and talking about how dumb and stupid we were and how could we have done some shit like that. And if someone asked me what did I think about the verdict, I always said, 'Oh, that verdict was something else.' Because it was so fresh. I was running. I was literally running to get away. Here's the media all in front of the house. Here's your neighbors all lined up waiting to see your face. It's just too much to handle."

And once you start trying to take it all in—the reaction, the way people are treating you—other things start crossing your mind. Whether you like it or not, you're constantly reacting. Don't forget, you've been institutionalized all this time. And when you get out and you hear all these negative things, the negative thoughts start coming in. I find myself thinking, *What if I get stopped by the L.A.P.D. or the sheriff and they remember my name? What type of reaction am I going to get from this sheriff or this police officer?* They seem to feel that we totally downplayed the L.A.P.D. serology lab and all this stuff. I know how things work in life—these organizations stick together. But what does that mean for me?

Carrie understood how I felt. "There are so many things you feel at once. What makes it so difficult is that you've been away so long that just trying to get back to normal is a big enough job. I've read a lot of newspapers since I've been out. I was so glad to see a full newspaper, I didn't know how to act at first. Because most of the time our newspaper was contoured for us, cut out. There was a lot in the newspaper regarding people's opinions about the verdict. They spoke out on those. That's how I familiarized myself. I went home after I got back from Vegas with my two children. I worked in my house, cleaning it for five days. I didn't even think to turn on the TV or the radio or pick up the phone because I wasn't used to having it. So you don't turn these things on because this wasn't something that you could use. For nine months you didn't turn on the TV. You didn't listen to a radio. You didn't dial a telephone. You just did what you'd been doing. This is what I'm saying about being able to get back into the swing of things. Right now I cannot use my remote on my TV because I don't know how to program it. So I have to use two remotes. One to turn on my TV and one to turn on my cable box because I have yet to slow down enough to be able to program it and remember my code that goes into it. I don't even remember my phone number. All these things I've got put away that I've got to go and get. Nothing is turned on. In other words, I really haven't adjusted. I'm still up in the air."

"So much has changed. Since I've been out on the highways again, I've noticed a lot of cars are driving with their headlights on," Marsha adds. "My husband rented a car when he came. I noticed it then. The lights stayed on. I kept asking, 'Why don't you turn off the lights?' He said, 'Oh, this is a new thing.' That was something new to me since I had been sequestered. I guess it's the '96 models that came out with that. As far as new TV programs, I had knowledge of them but I had not seen them. We would get the entertainment section of the newspaper. You couldn't get a TV listing but you could get the listing of new TV programs coming out or the new movies. We knew they were out there, but we had not seen them. So just dealing with some of the most basic issues in life is presenting a challenge that we never anticipated."

The way I see it, I'm the one on trial now. We all are. O.J.'s running around having a ball and here we are. We're the ones on trial. The people that have you on trial don't even know you. They just know of a position that you held. It's just not fair judgment. It puts you in an impossible situation. When I began I trusted in the court system, in the county. And you feel that they let you down because I think we should have been made a little bit more aware of what to expect and maybe situations should have come about where we would not have had to expect this. They should have made arrangements, and I'm sure they could have made arrangements, to relocate people. No one told me, "Armanda, when you get out of here, I expect your whole street will be covered with people and they're going to be attacking you. Now that you've done your duty, the county would like to give you a chance to get your life together and get back to your job." I know this is an extraordinary scenario, but no one took extraordinary steps to see that we were treated fairly after the fact.

A slew of things have happened to me since the verdict. I've been bombarded by the media, received a flurry of telephone calls, and hear comments endlessly everywhere I go. There are people out there who think I have actually made millions of dollars, and when people think you have all this money, they look at you a little bit different. No matter how often you say "No, that is not true," they're still going to believe what they're going to believe. This situation has corrupted my whole lifestyle. Not that it was a great lifestyle to begin with, but it was great to me. It appears that it will never be the same. This trial is going to be with me and a part of me. I don't know how long, but it looks like it may be a lot longer than I ever anticipated it to be. Sometimes I sit alone and say to myself, "How did I get here?"

3

ARMANDA COOLEY

If asked to describe myself I would say I am a very take-charge, self-sufficient, go-getter type of individual. I was born March 15, 1944, in East Chicago, Indiana, a small town just 10 miles outside of Gary, Indiana, and about 25 miles from Chicago, Illinois. I am the oldest of my mother's six children. My brother Sherman, who is now deceased, and I were the products of my mother's first marriage. I have four other siblings, a sister and three brothers, from my mother's second marriage. One brother resides in Ontario, California, and the other three siblings are still in East Chicago. My mother is currently living in Detroit, Michigan. My father passed away in the early 1980s.

I was raised by my grandmother, who took me from my mom shortly after birth because Grandmother felt she was more responsible and able to handle the raising of children than my mother was. Throughout my life I called my grandmother "Mom." She did not work. She was married about four or five times and was a housewife. She had owned rental property, which served as her income.

I lived across the tracks in a predominantly black neighborhood. There were some whites who went to school with us. The white kids let you know that being white carried some type of superiority.

There were certain cities in Indiana we could not live in, such as Griffith and Highland, during that period of time. Where I grew up we were not even allowed to go to certain stores. When I went to certain stores, the salespeople would look at me like they knew I was stealing something, and while they're looking at me thinking I'm stealing something, the white kids got it and gone. Let's not forget, I was brought up in the sixties during the militant years. I probably thought I was just as militant as the next one. Maybe just as much as my grandmother would allow me to be.

It's so important to eliminate racism starting from the cradle. We have to start with our children because that's when they're most impressionable. When children are not aware there's a difference, you see a lot more happiness and a lot more peace in their lives.

Back in that particular time and place you were sort of raised by everybody. There was nothing that you couldn't do that the neighbors wouldn't scold you for because they all looked after us and insisted on proper behavior. If a neighbor did scold you and it got back to your parents, you were as good as dead. I grew up thinking I was poor because it seemed white kids always had more than me. I think that came about from listening to people talk in the neighborhood. I didn't realize that I wasn't truly poor until I was an adult. We ate well everyday. Even if we had beans, we had some fried chicken or something else to go with it. I never went barefoot. Like I said, I was an adult before I realized that I truly lived well. We were brought up in a church environment. Every Sunday I went to Sunday school. I spent the day in church with Bible training and a session in the evening.

I had a happy childhood, although I really didn't realize it until I was fully grown. I think about it now. All the roasts I ate. All the peach cobblers and all the four-layer cakes. Jelly sandwiches. And we only ate those because you wanted to eat them. But you didn't have to because there was other food there and lots of it. As an adult, I tried to realize what made me think we were poor in terms of not having what other children had. I mean, there were always the affluent blacks, the lawyers and the doctors, who lived in the nice big houses and drove the nice big cars. You always had those in the neighborhood. But their kids went to the same school I went to, which was a public school.

My upbringing was strict. As a child, I sometimes resented my grandmother, but I now realize that she did a wonderful job giving me a strong sense of family and responsibility. Lying was something that Grandmother hated more than anything. She would punish me mightily for breaking this commandment. To this day, I have a scar on my leg where she beat me for lying to her about going to the movie theater in Hammond without permission. It was more of an adventure to see the movies in Hammond because that's where the teenagers would go, especially the teenage boys. But my brothers and sister had to go with me, and that put a damper on being able to talk to the boys. On that occasion, I had made my siblings promise not to tell Grandmother where we had gone. Unfortunately, I left my wallet in my seat and the theater sent the wallet home. When Grandmother approached me about what movie I had seen, I lied. We made sure we knew what was playing at the neighborhood theater so that we'd be ready for this question. When she pulled out the wallet, that was it. Next she pulled out the extension cord and took me to the bathroom for a lengthy whipping. That's the only time she punished me like that. For two years after that I was not allowed to go to the movies.

I was not even allowed to date until I was sixteen years old. There were boys you played with in the neighborhood, but they were just friends. There was nobody I had the hots for or liked in any kind of way, although I did manage to once again fall into the trap of lying to my grandmother.

I must have been about fifteen years old when I sneaked out of the house one time to go to one of the teenage hot spots. My friends were allowed to go to these parties but I wasn't. There I was just dancing away and who taps me on my shoulder but my grandmother. She snatches me up by the collar and drags me out of there. That was the last hot spot I went to because I was totally embarrassed after that episode.

Grandmother truly had a thing about lying. That was the worst thing you could do. I would often wonder if it was the worst thing you could do because even if you told the truth, you still got killed. The whippings my grandmother put on me would probably get somebody put in jail today for child abuse.

I recall when I broke another one of the Ten Commandments. I stole some money from Grandmother's purse. I had asked her for the money but she said she didn't have it. I knew she had a purse full of money so I took $20. That was a lot of money in the 1950s. I dashed to the candy store and presented the $20 to the shopkeeper. The shopkeeper called my grandmother to tell her what I was doing. That was all she wrote when I got home.

My grandmother had a look that could terrify you about what was coming next. When she put the look on you it was worse than anything. You'd shake in your boots all day, worried to go home. She knew how bad I hated staying in the house so she would punish me with detention more often than with whippings.

Every Fourth of July brings back the memory of almost burning Grandmother's house down. My brother Gary has always had this vision problem and wore these thick glasses. We had brought some sparklers for the Fourth of July. My grandmother said not to burn the sparklers in the basement. Wait until nightfall and then go outside. We went down there and burned them anyway. I told Gary to stand still while I lit them. I turned to light my other brothers' sparklers. At the same time Gary turned and accidentally set the curtains on fire. We burned down the basement.

I graduated from high school in January of 1962 and took a few business courses at Indiana University Extension. My high school sweetheart, Lawrence "Zeke" Cooley, and I were married on February 15, 1965. I was a virgin when I married. I'm telling you, my grandmother would put the fear of God in you. When she said, "Keep your dress down and your drawers up," you could not think in terms of doing anything because you could just see and hear her.

Zeke had enlisted in the Marines in 1961 and was shipped to Vietnam shortly after our wedding. I stayed in Indiana but not with my grandmother. At that time I was out on my own. I worked as a receptionist for a pediatrician for several years after my marriage until Zeke was out of the service. While he was in the service, we moved to various areas where he was stationed. Eventually, we moved to Los Angeles in July of 1975. We had one daughter, Yolanda, who was born April 9, 1967, in Seaside, California. When my husband came out of the war, Yolanda was about eight months old. In Los Angeles I gained employment at a company called Carte Blanche, which later merged with Diners Club. I worked there for about seven years. In 1978 Zeke and I separated due to his alcoholism and the traumatic effects he experienced from the Vietnam War. Zeke moved back to East Chicago, Indiana, where he currently resides. In September 1991 I filed for divorce.

We never had any type of abusive relationship. Just like anybody else, we had verbal arguments but nothing physical, so I cannot relate to that other than through people I knew who were in abusive relationships. Basically, I could not see myself even staying in a relationship like that. That's the reason why I can't understand why people think because you are black and from South Central that you can relate to these types of situations. I mean, that's not true at all.

I then went to work for a retail outlet, The May Company, in the credit collection field. I am presently an administrative assistant III responsible for monitoring the outside collection agency contracts. When the county refers to outside collection agencies under contract, I ensure that the contracts are governed by the rules and regulations set up by the state and the county. This will be my twelfth year in the collection business with the county.

As I said, my mother and father were separated. I had a real problem with my father growing up because he was the type that would lie about coming to pick me up and take me on vacation. He would never appear. In the summer he would say he's going to take me south with him and I would pack up my stuff. My grandmother would come into my room and say, "What do you think you're doing? That man isn't coming." She never really had anything good to say about him. For years I thought she was the cruel one. I thought she was the one who kept him from picking me up, until I grew up and realized he was just a dog. Even when he died, I had a difficult time going to the funeral. My mom begged me to go for the sake of representing the family. I did it for that reason.

4

MARSHA RUBIN-JACKSON

I was raised in Oakland, California, in a neighborhood where we were one of the few black families. There were four children: my sister Linda, my brother Fred, myself, and my brother David. I was baptized a Catholic and was raised in a Catholic home. We attended church every Sunday. I went to Catholic school until the sixth grade, then I attended public schools. As far as being a devout Catholic, I am not. I have not attended church in a while. I still believe strongly in God and have always had faith that he would never put more on my shoulders than I could handle.

My sister was in the Black Panthers back in what I guess you call the hippie era. Because of our five-year age difference I wasn't privy to a lot of what Linda was involved in. I didn't know much about what was happening in that era. At times I still call her my love-child sister. We love each other dearly and I would do just about anything for her. She would come home and I'd be watching TV and she'd say, "You need to turn that boob tube off. You're just sitting here watching those white racist pigs." I would just look at her like she was absolutely crazy. "What are you talking about? I'm sitting here in my house while you're down there in some shack." The Panthers were talking about Power to the People, but I think they went about it all wrong. I wasn't caught up in all that hostility. I guess I was sheltered from it by my mother and father. They kept us away from it as much as they could.

I guess you could say I had an identity problem because I really didn't associate myself with the label "black." All my friends were white and Japanese. I wore a natural for a while one year because it was cool; it was a fashion trend. It wasn't a statement of political beliefs.

I was raised around mostly white people. I don't even have any rhythm. My husband teases me all the time about the way I dance. He says, "You just don't have any soul at all." I was at Venice Beach one day when one of the boardwalk entertainers pulled three women from the group of spectactors: a white girl, a Japanese girl, and me. He started dancing with this little white girl, portraying the way white people dance. Then he started dancing with this Japanese girl the way he thought Japanese dance. He gets to me and dances with me like he thought most black people do. I started dancing like the little white girl danced because I have no rhythm.

My father was a hard worker. He had his own barbershop so he wasn't at home much. My mother also worked every day. Sometimes she would work two jobs so that we could have piano lessons and ballet lessons and could attend good schools. We grew up as latchkey kids but were given the best of everything. My parents were always there for us.

I was a mama's girl. I wasn't out tumbling in weeds getting dirty. I was prissy. As a matter of fact, I was teased by my family, especially by my sister, Linda, for being so prissy. She had a name for me. I can't remember exactly what it was. Little Miss something. She still calls me that with affection.

My brothers and I have a loving relationship. Of course, being siblings, we often had arguments growing up in the same house. It was okay if we fought among ourselves but God help anyone who got between us. I'm real family oriented. Wrong or right, I'm behind them. This is the way I was raised. I had a great childhood. As far back as I can remember, I never really needed or wanted for anything.

Mother wasn't quite as strict with me or my younger brother as she was with my older sister. My sister couldn't date until she was fifteen or sixteen years old. I was allowed to have my friends to the house. When my little brother David came along, he was spoiled rotten like I was. David and I were real close and still are. Oftentimes, I feel like he's my son.

The most important life experience I've had was the birth of my son, Kevin Brown, on November 12, 1972. I became pregnant at the age of fifteen. This had been my first sexual encounter and I thought I was truly in love. At the time I was a student and I realized then that I would have to become an adult almost overnight. I had no idea how I was going to provide for my son. I wasn't even sure I would be able to go back to school and finish my education. Though I believe I disappointed my mother and father by getting pregnant, they stood by me. I remember walking past my dad one day late in my pregnancy when I was really big. He just kind of shook his head. It made me sad. It just disappointed him. It really did. But he never turned his back on me. My mother showed me how to take care of my child. I knew that some girls had mothers who were so disappointed that their daughters were pregnant that the daughters would have to go away and have their babies alone. My mother never made me feel that way. She wanted me to stay in our home and have my child. My brother David used to call my son "we's baby." With my parents' help I was able to finish my schooling. I worked hard to provide Kevin a good home so that he could have all the things my parents had been able to give me.

Like I say, I was my mama's baby and spent all my time at home with her. On my mother's days off I would pretend to be sick so I could skip school and be with her. When I was twelve or thirteen, my mother put me on her checking account. I was into doing this family thing, being my mother's helper. My husband, Jack, said I got caught up in that and became pregnant so that I could have my own family. At times I probably tried to justify getting pregnant by saying that I wanted my own family. But I don't honestly think that was the reason. I think I got pregnant because I was doing the "wild thing."

I had a lot of friends growing up in Oakland. When I became pregnant, many of my girlfriends' mothers refused to allow them to continue our friendship. But the one that stayed with me through my pregnancy and remains my friend to this day is Sabrina Glenn. She has often been a pillar of strength for me and I hope I've been the same for her.

My mom influenced me most early in life. She was a strong, hard-working woman. She taught me to be strong and showed me that hard work, faith, and hope always prevail. Mother taught me to be independent, to rely on no one but myself, to have faith in myself. Her positive attitude has kept me going when I thought things were really bad. I always hold my head up high because of the belief she has in me. Her influence is still strong.

In 1975, at the age of nineteen, I moved to Hawaii with my mother. At this point in time my mother and father had separated, so Mother sold everything in the house and we left California. My sister, Linda, was already living in Hawaii. She had told us what a great place it was and convinced us to come there. In 1978 Linda was in a serious car accident. She suffered severe internal injuries and we didn't think she was going to make it. At that time we were living in Kona. My father, of course, rushed to Kona to keep the vigil. Linda recovered. My father ended up selling his barbershop business in Oakland and has remained in Hawaii ever since.

I did a lot of little odd jobs while in Hawaii: retail sales, cocktail waitress. I never did get the hang of being a cocktail waitress. Fortunately, I was getting financial assistance from the state of Hawaii. I worked the security checkpoint at the airport for HPA, the Hawaii Protective Association. Then I started working for the CETA program for the Kealakehe Elementary School until the program was discontinued. I moved to Honolulu, where I worked for the Air Force Exchange. That's where I met my present husband, Danny Jackson, who was stationed at the Air Force base there.

I've been married twice. My first husband wasn't my son's father. Kevin never called my first husband "Daddy." I took care of Kevin and was his father, mother, sister, and brother. That may be one of the reasons my first husband and I aren't together today.

I met my first husband, James Davis, while I was visiting my sister in Hawaii. This was before my mother and I moved there. James was in the Army. We spent an evening together. When I went back to California, he started writing. We lost contact for a while but when I moved to Hawaii in 1975, I looked him up. We started having a little romance even though he lived in Honolulu and I lived in Kona. Eventually Linda and I moved to Honolulu. We ended up sharing a place with James and her boyfriend. James and I got married in the judge's chambers in December of 1979. We stayed together until April of the following year when I found out he had betrayed me with another woman. I moved back to the Big Island and in with my parents. James came to see me right before the Army transferred him to Georgia. This was during the time that the madman Wayne Williams was abducting and killing little black kids in Georgia. James pleaded his case, asking me to go with him: "Oh, please, baby, please." I said, "The only way you'll ever get me to Georgia is in a pine box." Those were my last words to my husband James. He got on the plane. I waved goodbye to him. I've never seen him since. I finally filed for divorce in 1990. My divorce was final in October 1990 when I returned to California.

When I met Danny, I was separated from James but we were still married. Danny knew this the whole time we were together. In fact, Danny was also married at the time. I don't know what

Danny's marriage was all about back then. It's ironic that I met Danny in Hawaii because we are both from Oakland. We didn't know each other when we lived in Oakland. One day we were sitting at a club at the Air Force base in Hawaii and I mentioned to Danny that I had to go back to California for a reunion my family was having in Bakersfield, California. As we talked, we realized we had practically lived right around the corner from each other. It's amazing, but my father used to cut his hair when he was a little boy.

We married on March 31, 1994. Things are fabulous. My relationship with my husband, I assume, is like any other relationship. There are always ups and downs. We are often separated because he is in the service. Our get-togethers are always like reunions. We look forward to settling down in a new home and helping raise, or advising how to raise, our grandson. We look forward to the day when we can just sit back and relax and enjoy our retirement.

I do realize that a lot of times I get lazy or too complacent about improving things or accomplishing my goals in life. I always feel if it's not broken, don't fix it. But my husband always seems to give me that extra push. He tells me that I should just push a little harder to do something a little better or to do something a little different than I'm doing now. Many times I resent Danny pushing me because I think he's trying to make me something I'm not. I realize I have the potential to do a lot of things, but I just get lazy and self-satisfied. I do end up feeling grateful for his encouragement.

I never encountered any type of racism until I moved back to California from Hawaii. I've heard black people say, "Oh, the white people are holding me down. If it wasn't for the white people, I could do that." I always felt it was your own fault if you let anybody hold you down. In our family, my father and mother always raised me with the idea that I could do whatever I wanted and be whoever I wanted. If I didn't get to do it or be it, it was my own fault because they offered me the best of things. They were there to back me up. Still, no one can hold me down from doing anything I want to do. So, I don't understand people saying things like, "Jesus, if it wasn't for that person there, or if I wasn't black, or if I didn't look like this or I didn't have that, I would have had more." I don't understand that. It sounds like prejudice to me. I can't deal with that.

Carrie and Armanda have talked about what it was like growing up in a time when white people lived on one side of town and black people on the other. I never experienced that division. When they mention their experiences, it is difficult for me to relate to them. They look at me disbelievingly, as if to say, "Oh, come on."

I know there were problems back then in the South. Juror #165, Mr. Calhoun, always complained about being raised in the South and how the white man will hold you back if you let him. I used to laugh and joke with him until I finally realized he severely hated white people. He was one of the alternates. I had made up my mind that if he was there when we got to deliberations and would be making the decision with me, I would have to write a letter to the judge and tell him of this man's hatred for white people.

I don't understand how anyone could live with that much hate toward people. It would just eat me up if I had that much hatred in my heart. If all of my relatives were in one room, you would see an array of nationalities. We have white, German, Hispanic, Italian. We all love one another just because of the person as a whole, not because of his or her color or creed.

I don't have one particular hobby. I enjoy riding my bike and swimming. I read when I have to. I crochet. I spend a lot of time at home. I like keeping my house, redecorating it and just being there. I have lazy days, what's known as Marsha days when I may take bubble baths or give myself a pedicure. I may go get myself a manicure, go get my hair done. I just enjoy spending time on myself. I get great enjoyment spending time with my family; my brothers, my sister, my mother, my husband, my son, my grand-child, my grandnephew, my niece, my nephew. It's fun when we all get together and barbeque.

When I got my notification in August 1994, I was told to report to court on the twelfth or thirteenth of September. I had plans to go to Hawaii that September to be with my husband, who was stationed there. While I was in Hawaii, Danny said, "Oh, you'll probably get picked for the Simpson trial." It didn't occur to me that I could be selected as a juror on that trial. It was only when the attorneys started asking us about being sequestered that I began to realize I might be on that jury. Wasn't there another trial going on at the same time? Snoop Doggy Dog? I think that trial was coming up around the same time. We used to see him in the courthouse hallway while we were going through the jury selection process.

That day I went down to the Superior Court building in Los Angeles was the first time I'd ever driven around L.A. I live in Bellflower, south of Los Angeles, so I wasn't familiar at all with Los Angeles. I got lost trying to find the court. The courthouse on Commonwealth wasn't a criminal courts building so I'm thinking, *Well, I don't know what the hell I'm doing down here now.* I finally got to the Superior Court building in Downtown L.A. I didn't think I'd get selected for the jury because I had no previous experience. I hadn't watched the preliminary hearing or followed the story. And that's probably why I was selected. Even when the court clerk, Deirdre Robertson, said, "Would you please stand?" it still didn't dawn on me that I had been selected as a juror. I looked around, thinking, *We still have twelve other people here.* That's why I didn't think they had chosen the actual twelve to serve on the jury. Mrs. Robertson administered the oath. There were fifteen blacks out of the twenty-four jurors. However, I wasn't thinking about the racial mix. I was struck by the mix of men and women on the jury. I thought, *Damn. We're a bunch of women.* There were eighteen women. It didn't really hit me that it was for the O.J. trial until I got the papers that actually said *People v. O.J. Simpson.*

This jury experience hasn't changed my attitude or my outlook on the judicial system. I've never served on a jury before, so I have nothing to compare it with. I always believed in the judicial system, although I've never had to experience it at work. I never had to spend time in any type of courtroom. I've never gone to jail. I seldom follow trials. Anytime I've ever called the police, they were there. I myself haven't had any bad experiences with police officers. My son did have a mistaken identity experience last year. He was arrested for an outstanding warrant and it turned out that the man they wanted had the same name as my son. It was cleared up and has since been forgotten.

My goal in life was to be able to provide for my son by giving him a good home and a good education. I truly believe I have achieved that goal.

At this time in my life I'm working as a mail carrier for the U.S. Postal Service. I believe I will retire if, God willing, I am able to stay in good health. I still want to have a happy home and a happy life with my husband. That has not changed since I became a part of this trial. I truly believe, as I stated before, that I have achieved a lot. I've been able to hold down a good job, I have a beautiful grandson, and my husband and I are looking forward to buying a home. I am still a family-oriented person who loves being with my loved ones.

Serving as a juror on the Simpson trial made me lonely for my family. The lengthy separation was difficult to bear. I missed out on many happy times and didn't get to bond with my grandson, Kevin Jr. Now all I want to do is visit with my grandson to make up for lost time. He certainly didn't get to know who I was in his first year of life. I just want to be there for him whenever he needs me. I also want to be there for my husband, my son, and my family. I haven't any different feelings about myself now than I did before the Simpson trial. I always felt good about myself. I still feel good about myself. I'm a strong person. I feel I've accomplished all I've set out to do. I will continue to feel that way for the rest of my life.

5

CARRIE BESS

I was born in Caruthersville, Missouri, in 1941. My mother died when I was eight. I'd never seen her but twice. Her name was Flora Smith. My grandmother reared us. She was named Lulu Lewis but we called her Grandma Rudy. She was born in 1888 to a family by the name of McKenzie. This was her slave name.

It was six of us children, three girls and three boys. Grandma Rudy had eight children, so that made fourteen kids living in a house with three adults. Seventeen in one house, a little shot-down house as they called it. It was a scuffle. But we never missed a meal. We always respected people. We went to church every Sunday. We went to Sunday school. Now that I've gotten grown and look back, there are so many people who have so much room and much less people, but they don't have love and understanding and caring in their heart. They become selfish. Things like that.

My grandfather was Irish and Indian. Grandma Rudy was a Blackfoot Indian. I don't know exactly what all my father was. I just know what I am: a black American. My family has a lot of different nationalities and cultures. We've got gray eyes, blue eyes, people who are white and people who are jet-black. It doesn't mat-

ter, because one thing I was always told is we are all God's children. It makes no difference. The only reason our skin is different
is because of the area in which we live. I can stick to that. I can
live with that.

I'm a Baptist but I have no problem with any religion because
it's like the fingers on our hand. We're all going different ways but
we're all looking for the Lord. I never have been able to understand people saying this religion is the one you go to heaven with
or that religion is the one that you're not going to see God with.
I'm a firm believer that if you believe in the Lord thy God, whichever way you go to get there, that is the way you will end up.

My grandmother reared us the best that she could. Her means
of support was harvest. We'd pick cotton, chop cotton. I started
picking cotton at the age of six. I would pick up to 300 pounds of
cotton every day. My two brothers, James and Roy (Roy is deceased
now), and I would pick a bale of cotton a day. This was the means
of getting our school clothes and saving up our money for the
winter. And then during the winter, my brothers would go out and
do what they call snapping cotton where it was cold and ice and
snow were on the ground. We would bring home our money and
our grandmother would give us all the money we made on Saturday just to buy the things we would like to have, personal little
items. We all worked together. We ate together. We prayed together. Grandma Rudy knew how to make a way out of no way.
She used to bake rolls and do the laundry for the white people or
do all the scarves for the people at the funeral home. This is the
way that my grandmother took care of the six of us after my mom
died.

My oldest brother, Robert, who was in the Korean War, gave
us an allotment, which took care of me and my sister Ann. This
allotment enabled us to do better through the winter months.
When I was old enough to go to school, we would work during the
summer months and during the fall when we returned to school.
During the winter months we had nothing to do, just harvest. We

raised chickens. We had gardens. We slaughtered hogs. We did whatever means there were to survive during the winter months. In the wintertime I ran a pool hall for the owner. I did a lot of little things for money. For the neighbors I would gather the coal and wood. Grandma Rudy always told me it wasn't what you do, it's how you do it. It wasn't what you had, it was what you did with what you had. It wasn't how other people saw you, it was how you saw other people and treated them.

When I was growing up I got into a lot of fights. I used to get three whippings a day if I lost a fight. I fought every day. It wasn't about me wanting to fight every day. It was about defending my family. If my sister got in trouble, I had to help her. Then if they whipped the two of us, my other brother would come in. If they whipped him, then the other brother would come in. It was a big family and we stood up for each other.

Our house had cardboard walls. You could actually see daylight out of them. We paid $8 a month to live there. That's how long ago that was and how meager it was. We lived next door to the Causeys. Reverend Causey was a minister from Chicago. The kids would call our house "the little breezy house." When I started school the kids used to call us "the old raggedy Lewises" but we were clean every day. I was about seven when one day the Causeys said, "You all live in a raggedy house." So I took some great big matches and I started a fire in our house. I thought if I burned down our house we would move. I ran into the kitchen and told my grandmother that I needed a cup of water. I thought I could throw the cup of water on the fire and put it out. But by the time I got the water, the whole house was burning. The family came in and put it out. As my grandmother was telling me that she was going to whip me, my mother came up to the house in a cab. She told my brother to go and get three weeping-willow branches from the tree outside our house. She took her time and braided the branches. And when she finished, it was almost like a whip. She whipped me so long and so hard that its memory would keep me from ever setting anything on fire. My mother said she was coming back the next year to get my sister and me. But she died that year, on December 8, 1950.

I remember when I learned my mother had died. We were at the Stadium Theater and my brother came up there and said, "You have to come home because your mama's dead. Mama's dead." I started running home. I outran my brother on his bicycle because I was so fast. When I got home, my grandmother was sitting in the kitchen. I was relieved because I thought she was the one who had died. I thought of her as my mother. As I said, I had only seen my real mother twice.

We were always bad. We'd slip off and go swimming in the Mississippi River. Thrash somebody's fruit trees. I remember there were these great big hogs. Next thing you know we'd have a rope around the hogs and we'd be riding the hogs down the street. Other than that, I must say, I still had a very good life. My grandmother took time to teach us all the basic things in life: reading, writing, sewing, and cooking. She felt that if we learned these things, we could survive. Grandma Rudy also taught us that you didn't mistreat other people. You treated other people like you wanted to be treated. This is what has kept me motivated. I'm more than grateful for that.

I went to Washington High School in Missouri. My history teacher, Orville Waller, and my home economics teacher, Zelma Perry, also kept me motivated. They would take me under their wing every weekend or so and talk to me. They would give me extra classes and books to read. They did this so that I could improve myself and stay steadfast in accomplishing my goal. And I stayed with that. After finishing high school, I received a scholarship to Lincoln University in Jefferson City, Missouri. My main objective was to be able to go to college and become a modern dancer and a physical education teacher, and to give something back to my grandmother and my aunt, who had devoted everything, all their work and all their crying times and sacrifice, to us.

Unfortunately, at that point I met with the misfortune of becoming pregnant, and this was another turning point in my life. After getting pregnant with my son, Alfred Smith, I got married. I got a job working in a box factory making boxes. Working on keels. That was a very complicated job because you used frozen wood that comes on like flats and you had to keep that keel full of wood. I also worked as a nurse's aide in a clinic. I've done a lot of different things, including being a secretary at the school from which I graduated. I also worked at the Brown Shoe Company as a fancy stitcher in 1961.

Grandma Rudy and my auntie died fifteen days apart. In that same year my husband William Bess and I broke up. One day he jumped on me. That was it for me. Everything happened in the same year. So I said, forget Missouri. I had another child by this marriage, Romonia, who was one year old at the time. Alfred was five. I put my kids in the back of the car and I headed for California. My youngest brother came, too. I didn't have a job, but the school where I had worked as a secretary had given me three months' pay. I brought that along with me and I never went back to Missouri.

I worked two jobs at a time in Los Angeles and finally got a job as a clerk at the U.S. Postal Service. I've been there for twenty-three years. Four years after I started at the post office, I bought my first house. I'm thankful I own a little piece of property in Los Angeles. A few years ago I added on the apartment, where I live.

Even though I've done well, I still tell my kids I'm poor. But my daughter always tells me, "Mom, you're not poor. We're one of the richest families in the world." And I always ask her, "Why are others so well off?" She says, "Mom, we got love. We're not taking. We're not begging. We got a place to stay. We are very blessed. We may not have as much money as a lot of people. We might not have all this but we're truly blessed." I can understand it because I've been around a lot of people who had a lot more than me but they weren't as happy as I am. You are always trying to hold on to what you've got because you're scared somebody is coming up to get it. I mean, if you come and get what I have, I don't have anything. But if you ask me for it, I'll give it to you.

I've gone to school in Los Angeles. I went to the Los Angeles Trade Technical College and took a lot of accounting classes. I took an English class. Like I tell a lot of people, my speech may be a little different from yours, but if you listen to me, I'm sure you'll understand what I have to say. If there's a question, you can always ask me.

My goal in life, as I said earlier, was to finish college and become a physical education teacher and a modern dancer. My other goal was to raise my children away from the South so they could get a better education. I am grateful that they did. Also, I feel that my goals have become plans now. Although I did not reach my goal as a younger person, I'm working on a plan of being financially set so that I can retire before I become too old to enjoy life. I do not feel I have accomplished the goals that I set early in life, but I do feel I have met some of my plans in later life. One plan is to remodel my front house so that it looks like the apartment that I built in the back of it, change the windows, do the landscaping. These are the things I hope to do next year knowing that I will not be sequestered.

I also really need to regroup, to get back to my life as it was before the trial. I know that nothing will ever be the same because mentally I look at things totally differently. The experience has changed me to the point where I find that a lot of things I always thought were necessary, like my house having to be cleaned every week, are not. I always thought no one could survive without my being there.

My job is one of the most important things that I look forward to at the present time, other than being there for my children. This trial and being sequestered were significant to me because I had never left my children since the day they were born. That might seem strange. Sure, they have left me at times, but I have been stationary for my children all of their lives. My son, Alfred, is thirty-four and my daughter, Romonia, is twenty-nine.

As far as the upkeep on my property, the manicuring of my lawn, the caring of so many things, I find these things go on. There are so many times I wish I could recapture the hours I lost to maybe regroup, even think about getting married or doing things of that nature. But it has come to the point where those things right now are not important to me. The most important thing to me now is trying to adjust, trying to feel myself, trying to understand myself.

I haven't the patience that I used to have. My attitude toward things is totally different. When someone comes up to me and demands my presence or my attention, I want it to be of importance to me or to them. I just don't want to do idle time, and God help us if someone thinks I'll wait in an enclosed environment for them to do things. I really realize that I have changed tremendously. And I want to be able to relay my feelings to people without a problem. I want to be gentle. I want to be nice. I want to be the way my grandmother raised me. By the same token, I don't want to be controlled ever again by anyone.

There are just two of my siblings who are still living. My mom's dead. My father's dead. Strange as it may seem, I have yet to call anyone other than my closest friends, and there are only two of them. I did anticipate going to see my sister and brother, but when the weather changed, I delayed that plan. There are other things that have come up and delayed me. I must say that I long to see them. I want to feel that love. But that feeling of doing something you have to do, something that's demanded of you— when I think of that, it becomes difficult for me to agree to do anything. It's not that I don't love them. It's just hard for me to do something if I've *got* to do it.

While I was sequestered I lost my oldest sister. I really miss her. I flew back to Missouri on the red-eye, stayed there four hours, and flew back for the trial to keep from holding it up. She was buried the next day. I want to say thank you to Deputy Tokar for being with me when my sister died. Deputy Tokar flew home with me just so I would have someone close by at that time. This was the sister who helped raise me. She had twelve kids, so I have a host of nieces and nephews.

As a matter of fact, my oldest brother, who served in the Korean War, had nine kids. My sister next to him had twelve, as I mentioned. My brother next to her had seven. My youngest brother, who passed away, had nine. And my sister next to me had nine and I had two. And their children have children and some of their children's children have children. My family is huge. But I'm proudest of my two children, Alfred and Romonia.

My dear friends are David and Zora and Jerome Weathers, my neighbor Anita Johnson and, of course, Jean Bryant. She's the one I call my mother as of now. She has been my friend for more than fifteen years. These are the people who really still stand by me. They might not be there every day. We might not talk every day. But there has been no time that I have ever felt that they weren't in my corner or that I could not go to them. Jean Bryant is one of my tenants. We all call her Mama Jean because this is exactly what she is to us. Jerome and Zora, we fish a lot. We sit around and we chew the fat. These are the people who are important and have influenced my life.

My hobbies are dancing, fishing, and playing backgammon, checkers and cards. When I was a kid we used to play hopscotch and all the childhood games. What I consider fun now is picking up a couple of poles, grabbing a six-pack, and going to the ocean or to the Salton Sea with a group of friends. Or going to Las Vegas. Traveling. These are the things I truly enjoy.

My leisure time is spent taking care of my property. I paint, build things, tear down things, work in the garden, or work in my yard. I'm forever doing something around my place. And when

I'm not doing that, I crochet. While I was sequestered, I learned to crochet. I guess I will be adding this to my leisure time.

I would not like to serve on a jury again. It's not about not wanting to do my civic duty. It's about the people who are running the system. This has taught me a lesson. It makes no difference how your heart is. It makes no difference where your mind is. It makes no difference what the verdict is. The people on the outside looking in are the ones who have to criticize, take you apart, talk about your mind, about whether you're sane or insane. I would love to see those people, the media, the ones that stand on the outside and criticize us. I would love to see what their decision would have been after they have had the facts.

I do not have anything against the judicial system because it is something that is written. My problems with the system are with the people who are running the system. If the people who are running the system have a problem with the way things come out when they send jurors in to come up with a decision, then I have a problem with the judicial system. Maybe it should be changed. Maybe it's too old for the modern times. I do not know. I feel that the judicial system works, but some of the people who work with the judicial system do not.

6

WELCOME TO THE
INTER-CONTINENTAL

We were not warned what it would be like to be sequestered, and I think that was cruel. Maybe they didn't know what they were doing, but the court could have shared with us the plans they had before it all started. I grant you, things got a lot better as the months went by, and we soon realized that the Sheriff's Department could do only what they were instructed to do—that their whole purpose was to protect us from any type of influence concerning the case. But I think all of that could have been done with less difficulty and at less expense. Eventually, we started bypassing the Sheriff's Department and making requests directly to Judge Ito in writing. The main point is, it's just not fair when someone has that much control over your life. On the day we were to be sequestered, Michael Knox and his wife picked Marsha up at her home and the three of them went to Dodger Stadium, where we would then be taken to the hotel. Marsha and Michael had discovered that they lived near each other, so that arrangement worked out well. Michael's wife sometimes brought Marsha's mother with her on the family visits on Sundays.

It was pouring rain that Wednesday morning. Raining like hell.

When I got to the stadium I could feel all of the mixed emotions in the air. Many of the jurors and their loved ones were crying. Marsha and Carrie had hangovers from overindulging the night before. I think it was sort of a last hurrah. I lingered with the others until our luggage was loaded, which took quite some time. There were eighteen women among us and we had all packed for a stay of at least two months, so there was a significant amount of luggage. Three vans transported us to the hotel, taking us in two separate groups. It was an emotional sendoff because we didn't know exactly when we'd be able to talk to or see anyone again. All we knew was that we were going to a hotel and that we would have private rooms. We had no idea that we would not be able to talk on the telephone whenever we wanted to. Things that you ordinarily took for granted would be handled differently now. We had simply been told to pack, where to meet, and to be there on time. That was it. We weren't allowed to bring radios, but we could have CD players as long as they didn't have an AM/FM radio built into them. There was to be no uncensored news from the outside world.

At that time, I hadn't developed any feelings toward anyone, but we were all cordial to each other. When we got to the hotel, the men went in one room and the women went in another. Then they came in and told us how we were going to proceed: check in, line up, strip, and search. The sheriffs went through all of our items, and I think that we all felt that was the first sign of distrust. We already knew the rules and what we could not do, but they searched everything to make sure we didn't have radios, magazines, and any other prohibited items on the checklist we had been provided before we were picked up. It was sort of a prison lockdown type of situation—at least, that's what it felt like.

"None of us will ever forget the day we first gathered together as jurors to begin this trial," Marsha recalls. "We were at the court and Deirdre Robertson, the clerk, came in and said, 'Well, at this moment in time you are sequestered.' That was on Monday, the

Home for 267 days

Hotel Inter-Continental
5th Floor

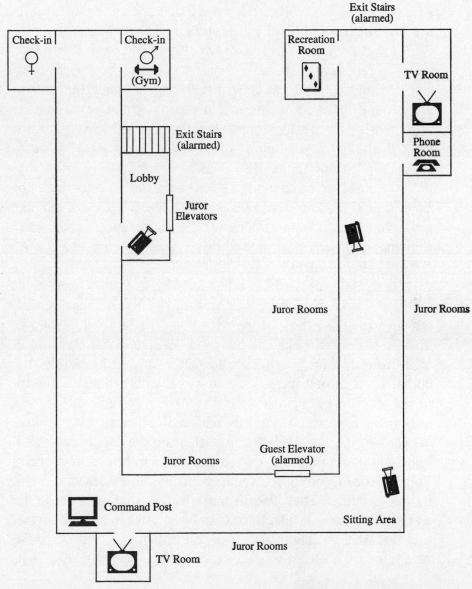

Exit Stairs
(alarmed)

Check-in ♀

Check-in ♂ ↔ (Gym)

Recreation Room ♦

TV Room 📺

Phone Room ☎

Exit Stairs (alarmed)

Lobby

Juror Elevators

Juror Rooms

Juror Rooms

Juror Rooms

Guest Elevator (alarmed)

Command Post

Sitting Area

TV Room

Juror Rooms

Video Surveillance Camera

ninth of January. Mrs. Robertson told us to go home and get our things together. We were to meet near Dodger Stadium on Wednesday, January 11.

"When I came home I had too many things to do," Marsha continues. "I needed to get my bags packed and figure out who was going to pay my bills. On Tuesday, I sat down with my mother to explain how to pay them. It wasn't that she couldn't do it. It was just putting a little too much pressure on her. I was thinking, *Well, I just bought a brand-new car.* I didn't know if they were going to repossess it, because I wasn't going to be able to take care of things while I was gone. I had already signed the papers given to me by the court stating that serving on the jury wouldn't be a hardship on me. I had wanted to start the bill-paying system through the bank, but I didn't have time to set it up—you can't set that up with no notice. There was such a mixture of emotions going on inside me. I thought, *I'll lose everything I have fixed up here.* Everything in my house is paid for. The only thing I did not pay in full is my car and I don't want it to be repossessed. I was thinking, *Oh, God. What have I done? This is going to kill me. I'm not going to be able to do this.*"

"I was quite surprised," says Carrie. "Things started happening a little at a time, but I thought it was nice at first because we had our own rooms. I thought we were going to be sharing rooms. Then to find out they had all this food. Man, I went from a size 9 or 10 to a 14 during sequestration. The only thing that really bothered me at first was we had to go eat whether we wanted to or not. Had to get up at five-thirty in the morning whether we were going anyplace or not. But that eventually changed."

The first day, we were getting settled and the deputy came and knocked on all our doors, telling us we had to line up for lunch. This was the beginning of an endless chain of lines we would form to do everything. They gave us more instructions on what to do and what not to do, when to do it and when not to do it. We were told that we'd be able to make telephone calls and that we could receive our mail from visitors on Saturdays and Sundays. That was a load off all our minds. I think some folks thought we were going to be cut off altogether, but once we found out the details there was a general feeling that perhaps we could maintain some autonomy while sequestered.

We were told that we could keep a diary or journal of our thoughts, but not about the case. Some of us wrote about our daily routine, how we felt, and the procedures we had to follow. And even though some of the jurors put on weight, the food at the hotel was not the best. We had to eat from a buffet setup and it was not first-rate. Later, when we got invited out to restaurants, you could choose to stay back at the hotel if you wanted. And when you stayed at the hotel by yourself, you could order room service instead of them making up the big buffet downstairs. Marsha was the first one to discover that—she skipped our first outing.

She told me, "When everyone left, I came out of my room. I was sitting up in the front TV room with the deputies. I ordered a steak dinner and they brought it up to me. The food was so much different from the food we were served in the buffet. I could not believe it. The food was cooked so much better when you got room service than when you were down there in the buffet."

Right after that, we received a letter saying that if we decided to stay at the hotel, we wouldn't be able to order room service. We had to eat whatever had been served at the buffet. A lot of times, the fish tasted stale, the chicken would be overfried, the steaks would be tough, and the bread and rolls would be cold. I will never forget that food. Everybody kept complaining about it, but they kept getting bigger and bigger in size.

The first couple of days we were filled with excitement because we really didn't know what the program was. But then the excitement started dwindling and we realized that we were no longer in control of what used to be our lives, that Judge Ito now controlled our lives, that the Sheriff's Department controlled our lives. And, no matter what, we were now part of the system. It was almost as if you thought you'd be shot if you tried to run away. It was the most depressing thing I have ever gone through, and I'll probably spend a lifetime trying to help others so they never have to go through that. It is cruel and inhumane punishment.

While we were busy adjusting to the rules, acquaintances were becoming friends and, in some cases, frictions also arose. For example, Jeanette and Marsha befriended each other but as time went on, they started drifting apart. Jeanette seemed to get along better with Sheila, who was really quiet. Marsha had always been able to entertain herself with mystery books her sister, Linda, brought her. That, or she worked on puzzles her husband gave her. When I realized her fascination with puzzles, I gave her a great big poster-sized puzzle to put together. Francine Florio-Bunten had even let her use a double-sided one, which was considered the world's most complicated puzzle to put together. She always kept herself busy.

Marsha admits, "I didn't get myself involved with a lot of the goings-on in the TV room or in the recreation room. A lot of times, I would hear things from others I did not know about firsthand, so I would not be able to comment on them. I'd hear about Willie and Lon in the TV room. Willie would tell the folks to be quiet. He was talking to grown people like they were crazy. I often thought to myself, *If I hadn't been able to entertain myself like that, would I also have been involved in a bunch of the trouble that happened on the fifth floor where we were sequestered?* I just stayed away from there. I just separated myself because I didn't want to be involved in any type of altercation with anyone. I knew that if I were in there and Willie was talking to me like I was his child, I'd have to cuss him out. I just separated myself from that, but I kept my ears open. As one of the jurors said, I'm always busy. I'm always in other folks' business. I'm just inquisitive. I like to know what's going on. That's all. I guess I'm nosy. I try to pay a lot of attention to what's going on around me, as I did in the trial. I paid a lot of attention in that trial."

"I guess we were all getting touchy, trying to get to know each other," says Carrie. "You get turned off by someone maybe saying something. Then they began to group off. People began to get in their own little groups. I found it depressing at times because I really didn't know anyone and I really wasn't close to anyone. I think people I was closest to are Marsha and Armanda. I guess you might say I was just the wild one. I didn't pick them. I didn't care where you were from or who you were. If you want to talk, let's talk. Let's run. Let's whatever. I enjoyed Francine. I hated to see her leave. We had a lot of time together. We would walk the beach and talk. I could talk about my problems and she could talk about hers. We had that rapport going. I ate with Brenda, Ann, and Gina every day. But that changed after a while. Then the jurors started dropping off. You'd be surprised at the privacy of our lives. We talked about everything. Well, I would not reveal some of the things that we talked about concerning our private lives. But we did talk about a lot of private things. I just want to say that some of our emotions go a lot deeper than you will ever know. I laid in bed many a night and cried because I wanted to leave but I didn't want to leave without my face. I didn't want to lose face. There were times when I was ticked off at the other jurors because I couldn't express myself or I felt like they didn't want me with them. I wanted to be "in." I wanted to sit with you. I wanted to talk with you. But a lot of time it just wasn't there. I couldn't find a place in any of the little groups. I was with everyone, but I wasn't with anyone.

"Eventually, I started hanging around the ladies who were doing the crocheting and I asked them to make me an afghan. I was doing macramé. The macramé was eating my hands up. I was making myself a purse, but the purse ended up looking like a hula skirt because I never put it together. It was just a bunch of strings. I asked them to make me one of those afghans they were working on—they were gorgeous. Marsha said, 'Ain't nobody gonna make you a damn thing. You want something, just make it yourself.'

And then Armanda said, 'Yeah, you go get you some yarn and learn how to do it.' So, I finally broke down and got some needle and yarn. I bought pink and blue first, but then I saw this pretty yarn. I thought it was pretty because it had a lot of different colors. But I was inexperienced. The others kept tearing it out and ripping it up. I was up to here with them tearing up my stuff. So I told them I wasn't going to stay up that night. I really felt bitchy so I said I was going to my room. But the real reason I was going was because I was hurt. They kept tearing out my crocheting. I went to my room and I said, 'Well, I can't let this defeat me. I have to learn this.' Armanda had told me if I wanted to learn to bring out that pink and blue yarn and they would help me. The next morning I did, and Marsha and Armanda were nice. They hugged me and let me know it was all right to feel bitchy and then they busted up laughing at me. Now, they'll probably tell you, 'Oh, she's feeling bitchy. She'll probably have to go to her room.' But I did learn how to crochet. And I was blessed. I made eight afghans. I made three rugs. These are things that you really learned to appreciate. It chewed up a lot of time for me. I was a fanatic, too. I couldn't go anywhere without my needle and my yarn. It really worked out. It really saved me a lot."

Midway through sequestration, Marsha and I started exercising in the mornings in the hotel gym. We would get up early in the morning because it was crowded with everybody wanting to get back into shape. By that time, there were only about eighteen of us left out of the original twenty-four. But there were only two bikes. I think they had a Nordic machine, a treadmill, and a stairstepper. We got up at five o'clock every morning because we were both early people. I'd be on the treadmill walking just as fast as I could and Marsha would be on the bicycle pedaling just as fast as she could because we thought we were going to lose weight. I had already gained five to ten pounds since I'd been there. We did this for a good three weeks straight. Boy, I tell you, every morning we'd be in the gym just working out. We were some health nuts.

I sprained my ankle one day fooling around, and Marsha kept catching colds and getting headaches.

Carrie teased us all the time. She had gained weight and we called her "Big Moon." We were able to laugh and joke and tease each other. At one point, Reyko, Francine, and Farron were going to be our aerobics teachers in an evening class we had organized in the back TV room. By this time, the front TV room had been opened up and the back TV room was not being used too much because they were showing the hotel movies, which everyone had already seen. So we had started using that room in the evenings for our aerobics. For a while, everybody would come in there and work out with us. But eventually the interest fizzled out.

The stress of the trial still showed through. Besides gaining weight, we all picked up little nervous twitches. I started biting my nails and often suffered from headaches, Brenda often suffered from headaches, and Marsha had gained weight and suffered from headaches, too. And sometimes I'd be sitting there and then, all of a sudden, I'd just start crying. I didn't know why and I couldn't explain it to my family or friends. Fortunately, I didn't have too many of those days.

I think a big problem was that there wasn't an opportunity to release the frustrations that we experienced. It would have been helpful to talk in a group, to talk about what had been troubling us, but we didn't have the time to do this and we didn't have the proper means to get such discussions going. Sometimes I thought that it would have helped if we could have had a glass of wine just to cool out and relieve some of the stress we were dealing with from sequestration and the trial. Even though I don't drink alcohol, I think some of the others would have benefited from a relaxing drink. We were adults, not children. I could understand limiting the consumption, but not banning alcohol completely.

Just thinking logically about it now, we probably could have done a better job with our mission if we hadn't had things on our minds concerning the conditions of sequestration. At times it was all very strenuous for us. So we tried to cope as best we could. Sometimes we didn't succeed in keeping ourselves together.

I had one of my little breakdowns when my daughter, Yolanda, was traumatized about being unemployed. I had to manipulate certain things to help her by paying her car note or her insurance so that she would not get depressed. I even relocated her for a month. I sent her to live with my sister back in East Chicago, Indiana, thinking, *Get out there. Go to Chicago and try to test that market and see how it is.* But my daughter's depression wound up causing me to be depressed. There wasn't anything I could do to help her or even cheer her up, and I could only call her at certain times and talk about it. But talking about it only made me more depressed and, after a day in court, I only wanted to hear about positive news. I even tried to stay away from people I knew were sick because I didn't want to hear about the details. I felt bad that I could not talk to these people, because I knew they just needed to hear a familiar voice from someone who would say, "It's going to be okay." But I didn't want to do that. I wanted to hear nothing but positive business because I was in a depressed state as it was. The people around me were so depressed that I felt I was spending the majority of my time trying to uplift everybody else.

I couldn't sleep one night and, I guess it was around two o'clock in the morning, I sat up and I just figured the hell with this. I have a life. I had a life before I came in here. I'm going to be in control of that life. What the hell can Judge Ito do to me? How bad can it be? I was willing to go to jail. How long would he have kept me in there? As long as he would have kept me on that jury? And that's what you feel when you're at that point. I got up and packed my bags, had my garment bag all zipped up. A moment of calm just sort of hit me and my subconscious was saying, "You can't do this." What stopped me was that I would have felt I was a quitter. Once I dedicated myself I gave my word to the U.S. Superior Court. And once I did that I had to follow through. I would not have been able to live with myself, and that was the only thing that calmed me down. I didn't unpack the bags until the next day after court, and I never mentioned it to anybody.

The only time I would even mention having depressing moments or depressing days was when I felt it was important for someone else's well-being. The others thought that I was so strong, the Rock of Gibraltar. It's important to know that the rock also crumbles and that I am human. I did spend a lot of my time talking and having conferences with the younger people because it was hard for them. There were some girls that had just gotten married and their husbands didn't understand what they were going through. They didn't know how to handle this situation, yet they didn't want to quit. But nobody in there was a quitter. No matter how we complained day after day, we still hung in there. We still tried to maintain the respect for the orders the court had given us about not doing certain things.

It was important that we knew we just needed each other. There was a certain strength we received from every person. For instance, little Annie, the white girl with the college degree, was such a sweet, honest little lady. Her whole family was. There was nothing pretentious. It was just her being honest and just being forthright, this sweet young lady. And through her, we were able to grasp onto a little of this honesty. Through Marsha, joy. We needed that joy and laughter in our lives to make it every day. Reyko and her husband were the same type of people. She was born and raised in Oregon. She didn't know anything about discrimination. You know, people are people. This is just how her family brought her up. And through her, we were able to grasp onto a little something else. Reyko is in an interracial relationship. It's a very honest one and a very sweet one. She was a very loving person. We could draw off some of that love.

We were able to draw a little something from each person that helped build inner strength, that helped you make it from day to day. There were days when people were upset, when they would just lose it, screaming and hollering and cursing. It was like, "The hell with this! I'm going to my room!" That type of behavior. But we were able to deal with it. We knew that that person was just having a bad day.

"My family and I had a problem sometimes when they would visit because I was nervous and tense and maybe my children were nervous and tense also," Carrie says. "Maybe I'd say something and they'd say something and I was very hurt. There was a time when I spoke to them and maybe they expected me to understand things that I just didn't understand. I didn't understand them. They didn't understand me. In fact, I have yet to be able to just sit down with my children and come to a real mother and son and daughter conversation with them since I've left sequestration."

"Being separated from my husband wasn't that hard for me because he is in the service and we are often separated for lengths of time," relates Marsha. "As it is, we basically only see each other maybe about every three to four months. So that wasn't real hard for me in the beginning. But the strain of sequestration caused me to miss him more than I would have had I been conducting my life as usual. It was the emotional need for support that made me feel his absence even more. There were times when I would be sitting there watching TV, and something would remind me of my family. Tears would come to my eyes. All of a sudden this real loneliness would just set in and I would just wish that I could go call my husband and just tell him how I was feeling. Many times when I'd be on the phone talking to him, there would be moments of silence. I didn't have anything to talk to him about at all. I would tell him that everyone was fine. I would want to tell him how I was actually feeling, but I knew I couldn't. A lot of our conversations would be short. Nothing exciting for me to tell him. We tried to laugh and keep each other happy. He really tried to keep me in good spirits, but a lot of times I would just ignore it and go on."

Marsha went on. "The hardest thing for me was not being able to see my newborn grandson. He lives two hours north of Los Angeles and I had made a promise to myself when he was born in September, not knowing that I would be sequestered in January, that I was going to get up there and see him as often as I could. I just bought a new car so I knew I would have been able to go back and forth as often as I could. I thought it was important that he know me. I thought that after I got sequestered, my son and his family would be able to come down and see me, but he had to work and he wasn't able to get down that often. So, here it is, my grandson is a year old and when I saw him two weeks ago after the trial was over, he didn't even know me. That was the worst part of this whole sequestration."

Most of the confrontations among us happened in the initial stages of sequestration. Tracy (T.K.) Kennedy seemed like the type that was dominating and accustomed to getting his way. I think he felt that the deputies were there for him and whatever he needed and wanted should be supplied to him. There were times when he would ask them to bring him a glass of water. Things like that.

As far as Willie was concerned, Willie had a dominating personality and maybe he was accustomed to intimidating people. Maybe he just has an intimidating personality. I've never had that problem with him. He's never approached me in that manner.

I heard about that incident when Willie would not allow Michael Knox to get on the elevator. I was not on that elevator when it happened—I was on the next one—so I really can't say what went on, but it was usually petty personality stuff. For instance, Mr. Calhoun always wanted to be the last one on the elevator so he could be the first one out. This way, he could be the first one in the van because he had a certain seat that he wanted to sit in. He would open the door for the ladies but he would be the first one jumping in that seat. That kind of petty little stuff. Some of the others would block him out of elevator. He would like to be the first one in the food line and they would block him out just to play silly little games. That's what happened some of the days. Those were the things that kept me going as far as laughter. Seeing a bunch of older adults playing those kinds of games is just funny.

T.K. and I had a confrontation once, and it was basically because of a miscommunication in terms of him thinking he was helping me. It happened when we first arrived at the hotel. I was still doing work for the County of Los Angeles. I responded to clients and did some contract monitoring while I was there because that's what helped pass my day. I needed a computer. The ruling was that we had to sign a letter with the court that we would not use our computer systems to store information regarding the case on the diskettes. T.K. was telling me how to write a letter to Judge Ito. But they had given another juror permission to maintain a daily journal and I told the deputies that was a double standard, because keeping a daily diary would mean there would be information kept about the case. What other information are they going to have in that daily diary? The case is their life right now. So what's the difference between my writing a daily diary on the diskette and someone else writing a daily diary in a notebook? I didn't understand that. But somehow T.K. thought I was downgrading him for trying to tell me or show me how to write a letter to the judge requesting permission for a computer. I later realized he kept this information on his mind for four or five weeks. And my approach to him was, if you ever have any problems with me or any miscommunication with me, I'd appreciate it if you would just talk to me rather than holding it in all this time, feeling that I downgraded you or disrespected you in any type of manner. Then, after we got that straight, he was excused from the jury for another reason.

T.K. had a habit of taking his shoes off at the dinner table. I didn't even sit at the dinner table with him. Nobody else seemed to approach him, but they would always talk about it out of his presence, and I eventually discussed it with him. He did have a superior attitude. Case in point, he was going to teach us how to play chess. When I walked into the room, he was teaching Francine and Catherine, who was the older woman dismissed early on, how to play. He was talking so rugged to them. "Well, how many times do I have to tell you that the pawn goes this way and the knight moves that way? And, I told you once before . . ." Very down and very degrading. At that moment I thought, *Oh no, I could not allow myself to sit here with this man because I would hurt his feelings. We would really have a problem.* Eventually, even Francine couldn't deal with him. Women of his own race couldn't deal with him. I don't know if it was a racist attitude, I don't think I'd call it that, but he did have a superior attitude.

"I had brought some dominoes and Michael and Tracy used to like to play them all the time," says Marsha. "That was the only reason I left them in that room. Actually, I didn't want anybody else to bother with them, but other people would go back there and play with them. Michael, Tracy, and Mr. Calhoun. That's who it was. And after Mr. Calhoun started acting like he was going berserk, I said I'd take them out of there if it wasn't for Michael and Tracy. Then, when they dismissed Michael, it was just Tracy and Mr. Calhoun playing those dominoes and I left them in there anyway. Then, when Tracy left, I went in there and took them and they started being rude to me.

"We'd be in the room watching TV and Willie would hold up his fists. I'm no TV watcher unless I'm watching an old movie or something, but I would hear all these stories about Willie and Lon, that they almost came to blows. I thought, *I'm not going in there. I'm going to keep myself away from there because if they say something to me, I'm going to go off.* There's no need to put myself in that predicament. If I can avoid it, let them have that TV room. Then, on a Saturday night when they were all off visiting, Armanda and I would go down and watch all the movies we wanted in peace and quiet. We'd laugh and talk and whatever.

That's the way we would do it. All during the week, we'd entertain ourselves. We hadn't started crocheting yet.

"I felt like Jeanette wasn't giving any respect, so why should anyone respect her?" Marsha continues. "She was a strong-willed woman. In the beginning, she was very nice. I have no problem with Jeanette, but she liked to stir up trouble. There was no need for her to stir up all this trouble. If there was a problem, it seemed like she should be able to talk to someone, but she often didn't. She didn't like Catherine at all. She used to tell me, 'If that crazy old lady hits me one more time, I'm gonna push her down.' The places where we could run outside to exercise were very crowded. After all, there were twenty-four of us. Anyway, they finally let us run around this little patio off the dining room and Catherine would walk real fast. She was a speed walker. And she was in good shape, as old as she was. She talked a lot—she was Irish and she would talk. She knew a lot about L.A. and I was very interested in a lot of things she had to say about the old L.A. If I would see that she would start talking too much, I would say, "Okay, Catherine. I'll see you later." She was a sweet lady and I didn't have to hang out with her, but I enjoyed talking with her sometimes. Jeanette just seemed not to like her at all. I didn't know why. Maybe she just didn't like her that particular day when Catherine bumped into her. Jeanette came into the dining room and told me, 'Yeah. She bumped into me out there. Next time she bumps into me, I'm going to push her down.' I just kind of shrugged it off. I just went on about my business. I had no idea that she and Sheila were going to go and get this lady dismissed. That lady did not run into her on purpose. I didn't understand that. Why would people run into her on purpose? That's what happened. We'd only been there for a little while and people immediately started complaining. I don't think they realized what was going on. I really don't think a lot of people realized you are sequestered. Sequestered means that you will be locked up, that you are totally segregated from the outside world. I don't think they realized what it meant when they signed the paper."

Once you get to know people you understand them better. Like when we found out that Lon's bad breath was due to the medication and the garlic pills he took. And he was aware of it, I guess, because he also used some type of breath freshener. I conversed with Lon. He was simply a person who was into himself. He was a part of the Vietnam War and a lot of guys who were in that war are still having problems today making it in society. He's so much of a loner. He's basically a nice guy, someone who enjoys his solitude. If we wanted him to sign a petition requesting something from the judge, he would not get involved. That's the first thing he would say: "No, I can't get involved with that. I won't get involved with that." I guess he was protecting his position on the jury.

And then there was Mr. Calhoun. Marsha could make Mr. Calhoun laugh; in fact, she was the one who started calling him Mister. There's no doubt about it—he was a racist who truly hated white people. He could be cold and insensitive to people's feelings. He didn't like David Aldana at all. But David always showed respect to him.

One of the big problems with sequestration is that you really don't know the people you're spending all of your time with, the people you're living with. You don't know their behavior patterns, you don't know their attitudes, you don't have any of that information. Basically, you've been thrown in with a bunch of strangers. But as time went on, you began to learn certain behavior patterns about your fellow jurors. Little things, like whether that person was a morning person or an evening person. Then you began to know their families and a little about the family problems that they may be having. And, as you begin to know people more and more, they begin to share more and more about themselves. That's what made it a lot easier. You could almost look at someone and know not to play with him or her that day. You would just leave them alone. And generally people who were having a bad day would go to their rooms and just relax.

Yolanda Crawford was a very emotional lady. She would almost have a nervous breakdown once a month. You could predict when those breakdowns were about to come. She was missing her mom, missing her life, and I could sense when she was about to break and knew when it was time to be supportive of her. I would give her the space that she needed at those times.

"It was tough, but a lot of lasting friendships did come out of being sequestered," says Marsha. "I truly believe that myself, Armanda, and Carrie will always be in touch. I think that Gina and Brenda will be in touch. We will also always be in touch with Yolanda and Reyko. Ann, #63, we got to get Ann married. We'll all be at her wedding. There's a lot of good that did come out of this. I do believe that if we had not been sequestered, we would have never, ever given each other the time of day. If we'd been able to go home every day and then come back, we would have sat there for our eight-hour workday and, as with anybody else you work with, said good morning and good evening. And that would have been it. I actually think I have found two very good friends in Armanda and in Carrie. I know that I will always be in touch with them and I will always be there for them because they were there for me. Those nine months we stuck together and we were there for each other. I'm sure it will always be the same for a lot of the other jurors also. We're just waiting to get back to our normal, everyday lives. I'm still feel like I'm in seclusion. It's like I'm just hiding out."

I don't think we ever got over the idea that we were being watched all the time. Some of us thought the blinking red light of the smoke detector was the eye of a camera monitoring the rooms. I know I thought that. I would purposely change my clothes in the bathroom so that I couldn't be viewed. Don't forget, there were cameras in the hallways, and a monitor displaying those areas was situated at the command post on our floor, so we became concerned that we might be watched inside our rooms, too.

"One day I got up in front of it buck naked," Marsha says. "I did. I shook my bootie. I said, 'Now, if you see something, I want to know.' I not only did that facing the red light, I did it facing the mirror, too. Late at night everything was real quiet and the walls were so thin, you could hear people using the bathroom. You could even smell the smoke when people would be smoking. There was a vent over the bathtub and if you stood up there by it, you could hear the people talking upstairs. At a certain point, I was thinking, *Well now, damn, if they are watching me, I'm gonna give them something to see.* One time Francine was standing out in the hall waiting for a deputy to open up the telephone room. She waited and finally turned to the camera and mooned it."

"I have a phobia and I just can't be waiting around. If nobody needs me, just don't tell me to wait in this room or hang around. I can't do it. Just can't. I need to get out," says Carrie. "If they have to sequester people, I think they should put them in an area where they would have freedom to walk around in the evening, as opposed to having to take them out everyday. Maybe if they could get a place where there is a courtyard, so you can walk around. We didn't have anything but those little hallways on the fifth floor to walk around. Marsha and I saw this movie the other day, *Assassins,* and there was a camera in the smoke detector watching a lady. So, how do we know we didn't have the same thing happening at the hotel?"

Of all the jurors who were dismissed, Tracy Hampton stood out because she seemed to have so many problems adjusting to sequestration. I knew Tracy was unhappy from the very beginning. I just knew she was. She just didn't want to be there. She really didn't. At all. It just disgusted her as far as I could tell. From watching her expressions, you could see how she felt. She and another juror would always ride together in the van. After that juror was dismissed, I think she was upset. That's when she kind of picked up with Michael Knox. She wouldn't talk to the rest of us. She had a real problem if she thought somebody might be giving her some real competition, and I think that's why she didn't talk to Reyko. Because Reyko was beautiful. Tracy played the role back and forth of the timid, helpless young lady.

Marsha says Tracy thought the male deputies were watching her. She was upset that there were no chain locks on our room doors. I felt she was paranoid and becoming more so each day. One day we were told that when the deputies knock on the door, they have to see you because they have to know that you're okay. They were responsible for us and if we did not answer, they would have the right to come into our rooms to check on us. So I think that's what happened with Tracy when a deputy entered her room. She did not answer the knock on her door because she was asleep and then panicked when she realized there was somebody else in the room. It was a female deputy who was just checking on her. Tracy even went so far as to think somebody was peeping through a picture on the wall in her room. But there was nobody in the room on the other side of her. That room was empty and locked. We didn't even start using that room until after this episode occurred and the empty room became a TV room.

"We were sitting at the table one day and she limped in," says Marsha. "She had hurt her knee. This was during the time we had all started gaining weight and Tracy got up to be about 140 pounds and I said, 'Tracy, you don't look it. But, I know what you mean, girl. I've gained about ten or fifteen pounds myself sitting around during this thing.' Anyway, she came in one day and she was limping. I said, 'Oh, what happened? You hurt your knee?' And she said, 'Yeah, I was in my room doing aerobics.' And I said, 'You fell? Well, sweetheart, you got to be careful.' And I thought that was that, but she kept sitting there and sitting there and then started coming to tears. I didn't know what was going on until she said that she really didn't hurt herself doing aerobics, that one of the deputies had come into her room and it had scared her so much she had jumped up out of the bed and hurt her knee.

"She was very flirtatious," Marsha continues. "She loved Deputy Jex. She'd say, 'I just love the way he talks.' After Michael left, then she took up with Mr. Calhoun and Willie. I remember one Saturday when we went to the beach in Marina del Rey. She and Sheila and Willie were walking together. On this particular day, Sheila came back to the van. It was windy and Tracy and Willie walked off to the beach. Willie had given his cap to put on her head. He had a coat on, one of those jackets with the hood, and a stick. I was calling him Moses. At any rate, they walked off, and they finally came back when it was time to go. Well, the next morning, the front TV room door was closed. I was coming from the gym area. I walked by and talked to whoever was at the central patrol, and I could catch a little voice coming out of that room. I just opened up the door and there sat Tracy and Sergeant Smith. As I opened the door, Sergeant Smith was facing me and Tracy turned. You could tell she had been crying. I shut the door. I made a little gesture to the deputy who was sitting at the desk there, as if to ask, *What's going on in there?* That night at dinner, Sergeant Smith came down and asked if there was any way possible we could help Tracy get away from Willie. He thought that Armanda and I could help, that we could talk to these people. More so Armanda than myself. I told him, 'Well, first, Sarge, you have to get Tracy away from Willie.' If we went somewhere, Tracy would always say, 'Is Willie going?' First she'd say, 'Is Sheila going?' Or she would come out and knock on Willie's door and ask, 'Are you going to dinner?' So what are we going to do to get him away from her?"

As time went on, we started to go on outings and see different things. One of the court clerks who worked for Judge Ito made arrangements with a lot of people. She used to write a lot of letters to get tickets for events. In the beginning we used to have entertainment on Saturdays at the courthouse. Now, imagine being in the hotel rooms and the court all week and then on Saturday the entertainment is held at the courthouse. You want to go, but then you don't want to go. This was during the time when you had the option not to join the activities if you chose not to. Then, of course, you would have to stay in your room at the hotel.

"We had an array of entertainment," Marsha recalls. "We had plays. One of them was called *The Imaginary Invalid* and another one was called *A Gentleman of Quality,* put on by two girls. *The Imaginary Invalid* wasn't too bad, but *A Gentleman of Quality* was one of the worst plays I'd ever seen in my life. There was a write-up in the newspaper about how the O.J. Simpson jurors enjoyed the play and gave them a standing ovation. This was when I realized the media can really twist things in the newspaper and magazines. There was no way in hell that happened, because the funny thing is, we hadn't even seen the play yet. I just happened to be looking in the newspaper one Sunday in the Entertainment section and I showed Deputy Tokar. I said, 'Did you see this? We haven't even seen this play yet.'

"Then one Saturday we had a trio play for us. It was a saxophonist, a drummer, and a piano player. It was called the Patty White Band. These people looked like they came from the Salvation Army. Anyway, this was a black trio. As soon as I walked in there, I started laughing. They played and we would clap whether it was good or bad. Then, another time, we had a comedian named Gary Nelson. All he talked about was potheads. He told some jokes that were outdated. It looked like he was high and a lot of his jokes referred to smoking dope. Well, I made a comment. I said, 'Gee, this kid is nothing but an old pothead.' And he had the nerve to give a few of the jurors his autograph. I couldn't believe it. I was told that he kept calling to come and entertain us again. We told the deputies, 'Don't ever have him back again!' Finally, we started complaining about going to the courthouse to see entertainment. So, Tessia had started getting us dinner engagements. Outdoor plans. Things were getting better. We went to the Biltmore to see Roger Williams, the famous pianist. The entertainment got better and better as time went on. We were able to get out more often. We rode in the Goodyear blimp. We had a boat cruise. A ship ride. Some rich guy had donated his yacht to us out in Marina del Rey. We went to the Pomona Fair. We went to a lot of dinner engagements. We went to museums. We got out. We had fun. We were able to get out to see every movie that came out. We saw all the first-run movies as soon as they came out—we would always have an invite. In fact, we had a lot of invites we had to turn down because so many were coming in.

"We were offered tickets to go on the ferry from Long Beach, California, to Catalina Island," Marsha continues. "We were going to have a tour of the island and have lunch. It was going to be a great day. We were going to go on a submarine boat ride where we would see the fish and how they feed them. I think everybody went. We all had our little summer outfits on. From living on the islands for such a long time, I've been on many charter boats. A lot of people were talking about taking Dramamine. I thought, *I won't need any Dramamine.* So we get on the boat and everything is going real well. The deputies were with us. It's a two-hour cruise over to the island. I'm sitting up top with Sergeant Smith. Deputy Smith, Deputy Browning, and Deputy Jex stayed downstairs. Deputy Long, Deputy Bashmakian, and Deputy Trauer were there and, as we get about halfway out to sea, they opened up the bar where you could get beer, wine, and sandwiches. They had given us a little coupon for a continental breakfast, you know, a roll, coffee. I go down and get myself a ham-and-cheese sandwich, a bag of potato chips, and a beer. In the meantime, Armanda, Bea, Carrie, and Yolanda are sitting downstairs. We were all over the boat because there were enough deputies for us to roam the boat. After eating my lunch, I was sitting there and about this time the boat started rocking. The water got real choppy. I've got sea legs. I'm all right. I'm laughing and joking and stuff. I hadn't even attempted to stand up because I noticed people were having a hard time trying to walk around the boat. A couple of jurors and deputies had taken some Dramamine. About forty-five minutes out from shore I started getting nauseous. I got up to go downstairs to the restroom. I got sick, sick, sick. Just my breakfast came up. But as I was exiting the restroom, I looked to the left and Carrie was sitting in the chair, just as sick as she could be. Armanda and Mr. Calhoun were all right. Sheila, Yolanda, and Brenda were all sick. So were Deputy Long, Deputy Trauer, and Deputy Dinwiddie. So, we finally get there. Things are going okay. We finally get our stomachs back. We have lunch. We have a good day, lots of fun. Until we get on that submarine. We were in close and there's no air. I started perspiring and getting nauseous again. Brenda had to get up and walk out and I followed right behind her. I got up on the deck and laid out in the sun until I was all right. But coming back, I died. It was too late to take the Dramamine. I was already sick. It was a wild ride.

"We used to go up to the old sheriff's training center to run around the track," Marsha recalls. That's the same place we went for pickup at the end of the trial. We were up there one day and I had on a red jogging suit. Deputy Russell usually moved real slow. We were walking around the track and we saw Deputy Russell running at full speed. We were so used to seeing him walk real slow that his running made us think something must be wrong. Then we heard the helicopters overhead. It sounded like they were landing right down on us. So we're thinking that the media found us. What was funny about the whole thing was when we got ready to get out of the van that day to run, there were some big paw prints in the mud. Deputy Mathews, one of the deputies who got excused, and Deputy Russell told us they were mountain lion prints. They said, 'If one walks up on you, don't run. Just hold your hand out like you're going to feed them because if you run, they get mad.' So all this is on my mind as we're walking. So when I see Deputy Russell running, I think, *Oh, Lord have mercy.* I took off running into some bushes."

"The only time we really had a bad experience was when we went to the Lakers vs. the Phoenix Suns game at the Forum," says Carrie. "We were recognized. A white guy started hollering. So they gathered us up and we left."

I'm not sure it was us that they recognized. Many times when we were out people would recognize the deputies from the televised trial proceedings. Particularly Deputy Jex. He was always sitting there in view of the camera. We were noticed in the Target store because someone recognized one of our deputies.

"The blimp ride was an outing that was arranged by Judge Ito," recalls Carrie. "As a matter of fact, when I went into his chambers, I thanked him for the trip on the blimp. He said his father-in-law had come up and wanted to ride the blimp so he called and, in the course of calling, he asked about the jurors getting a ride also. I think the blimp took about five or six at a time and it took three trips for everyone to get on. It's not as large as it seems. It had to be weight balanced. It was exciting because once we got up there they allowed us to steer the blimp, which is operated by the foot pedal as well as the wheel that makes it go up and down. The foot pedal makes it go forward. This was the last time we saw Deputy G12, because he died shortly after that, shot in a burglary of his neighbor's house. We called him G12 because he had a long Armenian name that began with a G and it had twelve letters in it. In the course of us riding, I was scared because I'm afraid of heights. But all of the others had gone up. I think the only one who did not go up was Francine. We're in the blimp with Sergeant Smith, G12, Deputy Smith, Marsha, and Bea. Bea's so afraid, she's not moving. Sergeant Smith is really hilarious. All he would say is, 'Holy shit.' And he had been in the Air Force. The pilot would take a nose dive and bring it back up. We all had a chance to fly it, but Bea didn't take her chance. Marsha was really into it. She flew over Long Beach where the trains are loaded and cars are brought in. On our way back Deputy Smith flew. The most memorable part of the ride came when G12 said, 'You're all up here thinking you're flying this.' "

"I want to say to the jurors who got dismissed early that it may not have been that good in the beginning, but toward the end sequestration did get better," admits Marsha. "I still would never wish it on anyone, though. We were able to make our doctor's appointments. We were able to make our nail appointments. When someone got sick, the deputies were right there. They got you out of there if someone needed to go home. Bea's husband had to go to the hospital one night and they were able to get her out to be with him."

Marsha went on to talk about the deputies who had been dismissed. "I wrote a letter to Judge Ito about the concerns I had about the dismissal of the three deputies. I sort of felt it was due to something Jeanette was stirring up. I couldn't quite put my finger on it. I knew she didn't like them. Then they were dismissed. So, you put two and two together. She was a hell-raiser. She could raise some hell. And I'm assuming that people found that out later, too. I wrote the letter and some of us wore black the next day. It was like we were at a funeral because we were all very sad. We had started to become a family. The deputies worked with us all day and all night. We started getting used to them. We weren't used to being locked up. We were able to start talking to these people. We were able to enjoy them. We could laugh and talk with them.

"Judge Ito called me into his office the next day and he asked me about the letter," Marsha continues. "He told me that he knew I felt very strongly about what I had written. I just told him that for people to get respect, you have to give it. I felt like Jeanette wasn't giving any respect, so why should anyone respect her?

"I called them my three deputies. This is the first time I'd ever been on jury duty. This is the first time I'd ever been sequestered. This is the first time I'd ever been away from my family and not been able to call them or talk to them when I wanted to. I was able to start talking to one of the deputies, Paula, about my grand-son, who I hadn't seen since Christmas, who I wouldn't see for a while, my mom, my dad, my sister, my brother. She would tell me about her wedding, how she'd be getting married in March and how she was ready to get out on the street, start going on patrol. She made arrangements for us to get our nails done, to get our pedicures. She made arrangements for us to get our hair cuts. She made arrangements for Jeanette's cousin to come down there and do our hair. I just couldn't see where Jeanette thought there was any type of racism going on. I knew that Anise and Francine didn't care too much particularly for Paula either. I don't know why. I know that Francine used to like to run and she wanted to get exercise. In the beginning, we weren't able to get out and get this exercise and I think Francine thought that Paula was just not doing it because she didn't want to. It wasn't that she couldn't do it, it was that she wasn't going to do it. She thought Paula was just trying to be mean. All this was new to the deputies also. They didn't know us. We didn't know them. They didn't know how we were going to react. They didn't know what to expect, and I don't blame them. I would have been a little leery with twenty-four peo-ple locked up on a floor, too. You can't just jump out there. You've got to kind of feel people out. A lot of things people referred to as racism, like they're doing more for that person than they're doing for me, that was just all bullshit. No one got to do anything that the other one didn't get to do. If you needed something, if you wanted something, all you had to do was ask. A lot of times it had been referred to as riding on folks' coattails. If I wanted to go somewhere or do something, I would ask. If I got to do it, then everybody wanted to do it. If somebody else wanted to do some-thing, I would say, 'Well, let's ask them.' It was all one big mutual thing with regard to the deputies and those jurors."

Although we never discussed the case among ourselves in compliance with Judge Ito's repeated admonition, we did develop a sense of humor about the attorneys and some of the members of the audience. At times, the evidence would cause laughter, as with the banana label found at the crime scene. One of the jurors was clowning around one day and stuck a banana label right in the middle of my forehead. After the Bruno Magli shoes came up in the trial, I was passing by Marsha's room one day and I took the box from a pair of Magli shoes I had and just threw it in her room. Stuff like that. There would be comical gestures made in reference to some detail of the trial. The only other things we would comment on would be whether that day in court was a good day or a bad day. This was the extent of discussing the trial. There were never discussions about the importance of testimony, evidence, or any development within the trial. Certainly we did not discuss anything concerning guilt or innocence. It would not surprise me to learn that there were discussions during conjugal visits, but if anyone did have them, they had the sense to keep them from the other jurors. Besides, as Carrie says, "They wouldn't do that because they never knew who was gonna say that someone told them something. So anyone who knew anything kept it to themselves because you would have jeopardized yourself. But as far as jurors hearing information from the outside during conjugal visits, I truly believe that if I had gotten any type of information while I was inside like what I've heard since being dismissed from the jury, I'd have had a severe problem with my verdict."

The only time I would be whispering or anything would be if I had some personal stuff on the telephone and you didn't want the world to hear about it. Other than that, we were institutionalized and we had the mentality of somebody who was institutionalized. And that would just sort of crack us up. We all knew where we were coming from.

But I really don't think that anybody wanted to hear anything. And if they did hear things, like Carrie said, they kept it to themselves. If I'd heard all this stuff I'm hearing now, it would have definitely affected me. I know that people find it hard to believe that we didn't talk about the case, and I can't confirm whether those who had conjugal visits did or didn't discuss the case. But I'll tell you this: Even if they did, you still have to trust people to be able to make a decision based on what they're hearing here and now. And I think we had enough of that and we were drilled enough so that we could separate what we heard outside versus in the bedroom. You have to trust people to be able to do the right thing. It's as simple as that.

I didn't have a lot of conjugal visits. Maybe I had about four or five visits the whole time. We felt, oh, we're saying nothing in here because the place is probably bugged. Nothing. That's the way we felt, so we didn't want to jeopardize ourselves. There were papers we had signed regarding things that would cause us trouble if we violated the rules.

"My mother would come to visit and she would say, 'Marsha,' and lean in toward me to tell me something. It might be something about my family that she thought I didn't want anyone else to hear. And I'd say, 'Mama, if you've got to whisper, don't say it.' And she'd say, 'Oh, no, baby, I wouldn't tell you anything about the trial. I'm getting ready to tell you something about what's happening at the house.' So I'd say, 'Just say it. Let everybody hear it.' "

You had dedicated yourself to this cause and you did not want to jeopardize your position. Don't forget, as jurors were being dismissed from the jury, we didn't know what the hell was going on. We didn't know what they were being dismissed for.

Sequestration is something that needs to be taken as it comes. There's no set way to do it. It's a day-by-day thing. Each day you have to get up and approach it in a different manner. I prayed every day. I prayed that I could maintain my sanity and that I could help somebody else to maintain theirs. And, hopefully, it will flow down so that someone else would help the next person and so on. Basically, that's how I was able to get through it. But some days I didn't think I would be able to do it. I'm thinking,

Oh, it'll be over in March. Then March comes and I'm thinking, *I'll give them until June.* And they kept going on and on. In one of the conversations we had with Judge Ito, he indicated that we'd probably be home by August. Then August came and went.

Now that I am out, I realize the importance of being sequestered, especially in this case. But I personally feel that with the money the county had spent, we could have had our own personal deputy on a twenty-four-hour clock staying with us. If not that, then give the jurors the opportunity to go home maybe once or twice a month. If you could just go home and see that things are okay, you could ease your mind. Or if you could just make a few changes or make a few quick phone calls, you could feel you were taking care of business. You don't want to sit there and have the whole world hear you taking care of your business over the telephone. Considering what we did and how long It took, I don't think that's too much to ask.

7

A TRAIL OF EVIDENCE

Whenever I sat in the courtroom I made a conscious attempt not to make eye contact with O.J. The only ones I made eye contact with were the attorneys and the media. I started doing that in the latter part of the trial. At first I tried to keep my head down but I started getting knots in the back of my neck. One day I just happened to catch O.J.'s eye. I truly, truly, truly just wanted to ask, "Did you do this? Did you absolutely do this?" I looked at him and I would just turn my head. He would get like a little slight smile. Just slight.

—MARSHA RUBIN-JACKSON

THE TRIAL

He killed her out of jealousy, Christopher Darden tells the jury during the prosecution's opening statements on January 23, 1995. "He killed her because he couldn't have her."

At the beginning, we were all anxious to get the trial under way. Remember, we had been sequestered on January 11 and not much

87

started happening until ten days later. I remember feeling glad we were going to court because we had been sitting in the hotel from the eleventh on, waiting and waiting. So when we found out we were going to go, everyone was happy. It seemed like we all felt a sense of relief when Chris Darden began opening statements for the prosecution. Well, relief wasn't the only thing we felt—or at least I didn't. When the District Attorney's office first sent Chris Darden down, I remember thinking he was there as a token because the jury was predominantly black. I thought the prosecution felt they needed this particular balance. To me, this was the first "race card," as it has come to be called, and it was played by the prosecution. It didn't fool me and it didn't fool a lot of other people on the jury either. But those feelings aside, I was always proud that Chris worked on the case.

Another thing I wasn't quite sure of was what happened to that attorney, Bill Hodgman. Was he sick or something? I sort of felt, *Well, why did they throw Chris up in here?* Was it because they looked around and saw the jury was predominantly black and they threw him up thinking we can get a balance up here? Like, well, Chris, maybe you can communicate with them things that we are not able to communicate to them. This is what I was thinking to myself because I know the games people play. I was just hoping that we had not gotten to that point in this day and age and that this was the way the rest of the trial was going to go.

I thought all the attorneys were great in their own way. I really did. But I sort of felt that Chris was a little down. Maybe he was playing down. I don't know. He did not have that upbeat mentality. I thought he was very moody. He never could look you in the

---

TRIAL HIGHLIGHTS

Week of January 9th, 1995 • Sequestration begins • **Week of January 16th** • Judge Ito dismisses two jurors: a woman (a thirty-eight year old Latina postal

eye, either. Because when I would look at him some days, his eyes would sort of look the other way. I have a problem with people who can't look me in the eye. I don't know why. It's just a personal thing.

But everyone has his or her own approach. And it was hard to focus on the personalities early on. There was a lot to absorb, like when Johnnie Cochran explained the difference between direct and circumstantial evidence. I remember my first feelings were nervous. You didn't know what was expected of you and you're trying to take it all in and then there were all these people sitting over there staring at you. It was an eerie type of feeling.

"I'll say," Marsha adds. "It took me a long time to regulate my breathing, especially on the first day. But I was able to settle down a little just after lunch. That first morning when I walked in there it was really hard."

We were being watched from the hallway on in. When we came through the hallway, they stared at you—everyone, the deputies, the media, the families, the spectators who came in for the day. When we went through the court and into the ninth-floor deliberation room and then came back into the courtroom, we were being watched all the time. We eventually got used to it—or maybe everyone just got used to seeing us—but it was unnerving at first.

Carrie adds, "When we first came through the door, there was a line on the side and, as we made that turn, there was a line in front of us. We had the media and the spectators in front of us and in the back of us. At first, they were allowing the cameras to be right there. They weren't focused on us, but it was a little

worker) who had previously been involved in an abusive relationship and a man who had met O.J. Simpson as an employee of Hertz. • Judge Ito rules that the jury will be allowed to hear allegations that

intimidating. These were the things that we remember. It's sort of hard to explain, but we never knew what to expect. Everything was so new."

Then opening arguments started. There was a lot that was said in those opening arguments on both sides and it was hard to remember it all later—what they said they were going to tell you about and later did, and what they mentioned and then never introduced as evidence.

"I remember, when Johnnie Cochran dropped his pen on the floor during opening arguments to show how deceiving circumstantial evidence can be," says Carrie. "They had a box down there and he said, 'Where did the pen fall?' This was how he was building his case to say circumstantial evidence wasn't foolproof. You weren't sure where it went, but you knew it dropped. Where did the pen go? You could hear it, but you weren't sure whether it hit the floor or the box. It was a little confusing at first. I think we were all nervous."

There was a lot of that. And there are a lot of ways you can look at circumstantial evidence. Like when a person lives by himself and he's up in his room sleeping, you don't have anyone to testify as to whether he wasn't home or he was home. It was also brought up that O.J. was noted to be chipping golf balls out back. I looked at it as, okay, how do we know if he does chip golf balls? I don't know. He was supposed to be bringing his golf gear to Chicago, but he could have had a club or something and hit a ball. I don't know. It's not for me to guess. But you can think about things like this. Is it possible? Have you been known to do this?

O.J. Simpson abused his wife, and listen to a 911 call made by Nicole. • **Week of January 23rd** • Judge Ito rules that the defense could cross-examine Fuhrman about allegedly racial comments

One of the first things you realize when you're listening to all this testimony is that you have to keep using your common sense.

> *"That's not why I'm doing this, Mr. Douglas. I'm doing this for my conscience. I will not have the blood of Nicole on Ron Shipp."*
>
> —Former L.A. policeman and Simpson family friend Ron Shipp

Very early on in the trial the witnesses were primarily Los Angeles police officers and detectives with the exception of Ron Shipp who stood out to all of us.

I felt Ron basically saw an opportunity where he could make money, and I felt that he was lying about that dream. His testimony was that O.J. said he had a dream in which he killed Nicole. My question to Ron is, "If he's your best friend and he's been your friend for twenty-something years, basically, I would not have let it just lie there. I would have asked questions regarding that dream. Like, what do you mean you had a dream about killing your wife? What exactly happened in that dream? I would have tried to get some details.

Ron Shipp is someone most of us didn't believe for a number of reasons. He appeared to be an alcoholic and I think he was a groupie. I seriously do. I'm not going to say I don't believe the part about the dream, but to me, his testimony was all about notoriety. That's what I thought. I really thought he was trying to cash in. And because of that I couldn't put any weight on the dream

he made to Kathleen Bell in 1985 or 1986. • Marcia Clark and Christopher Darden make their opening statements, starting by detailing a 1989 spousal battery charge. •

part and that was even before the family members' testimony about who Ron was and what had happened the night he spoke with O.J.

Now, O.J. could have told him he dreamed about killing Nicole. But to state that you followed him to the bedroom, or something like that, and then have the family on the other side saying, "No, he never was near him," that's a contradiction. Ron Shipp had said that O.J. and he had a chat and that's when he talked about the dream and all that. But why didn't he say something right then? He wasn't an officer at the time, but he was really good friends with Nicole. And then the family says, "Well, Shipp never did leave—he wasn't in there with O.J. alone." And then Shipp gets turned around and gets frustrated. I'm watching this and thinking, *Don't blow it out of the water because we're listening to you. You're emotional now. Come on, what's the matter here? Are you telling us this just because you're mad at him now? What's up?*

"I know Ron Shipp used to go by O.J.'s and he used to run people by there that he knew, but I discredit Ron Shipp for two reasons," Carrie points out. "Number one, after he got irritated there, he jumps and says, 'O.J. just wants to use people. That's all he wanted me around for. If he didn't have no use for me, that's why he kicked me out.' It looks like he's so angry that he'll say anything to get back at him. Like I'm saying, I was listening to each witness and thinking, *Where are you coming from? Are you going to discredit yourself in here?* Even though Ron Shipp had a drinking problem, it doesn't mean he wasn't telling the truth. Because in every bit of slander there's a trace of truth. But the point

Week of January 30th • An emotional Ron Shipp testifies that O.J. Simpson talked about dreaming of killing Nicole the day after she was killed. • The prosecution describes the contents of Nicole's

is whether you're going to pick the part that you need to pick out and stick to it. So I felt he was a liar."

"He had a very bizarre look in his eye, it was a very faraway look."

—Denise Brown testifying on how O.J. Simpson abused and humiliated his wife

After we heard from a few more officers, the prosecution began introducing testimony from some of Nicole Brown Simpson's family and friends. Denise Brown's testimony was the toughest to witness. While I felt Denise was a loving sister because it seems that she spent a lot of time with Nicole, it was difficult to understand how she would allow herself to get wrapped up in a lot of the emotional things O.J. was supposedly taking Nicole through—the verbal abuse and things like that. Because from what I understand, there were a lot of times she had seen things going on. He also put Denise out of the house, threw her out. But she kept coming back. I guess it's because she loved her sister that she wanted to be there with her. I didn't have any negative feelings toward Denise. . . . I felt that she was believable. But I also felt that somehow she lived a wild life herself. Alcohol, drugs, parties, that type of thing.

"The commander gave me a direct order that I should do everything I could to find Mr. Simpson and notify

safety deposit box, which contains photographs of her bruised face and letters from O.J. Simpson apologizing for beating her. • Denise Brown, Nicole's sister, tearfully testifies to the humiliation

him in person before the news media became aware of what happened," Detective Ron Phillips testifies on February 15. "He thought it would be very insensitive if we knew about it and did not notify him in person prior to the news media notifying him."

February 9—Robert Riske, the first officer to arrive at the Bundy crime scene in response to a 911 call, testifies that he saw the body of Nicole Simpson first, then Goldman's, and noticed that the door to Nicole Simpson's home was open.

During the first week of February we heard from various witnesses to establish the time line. We then began to hear testimony from the police officers who first arrived at the scene of the murders, like Robert Riske. He seemed to be an honest officer. He went in and did what his job was because he was the one who protected the integrity of the crime scene. Just listening to a lot of things that happened at the crime scene, I felt that he probably could have done a little better job but I guess he did the best that he could.

"Officer Riske could have made an error out there. There was blood everywhere. He could have walked in the blood when he stepped over the bodies and went into the house," says Carrie. "They just had a penlight. They said it illuminated a lot of things. But when you came back out of the house, out the door and into the gated entry area, the bodies were right there. They start right there at that step. It was tight there.

"And I didn't understand why he had to use the phone at the crime scene when he had radios. I know he said he used the phone

---

and physical abuse Nicole suffered at O.J.'s hands.
• **Week of February 6th** • A third juror is dismissed when it is revealed that she was a patient of a doctor who may testify. • The prosecution estimates the

because he felt that it was a high priority case and he didn't want to use the radio because others could have heard him on the airwaves. But then, as Johnnie Cochran stated, 'If you had not used that phone, we could have found out who she called last.' "

"He was one of the best witnesses they had," adds Marsha, "But I think he was very untrained. He wasn't trying to cover up. I just thought he wasn't trained well. He was the first one at the scene of a double murder and didn't know what to do."

Well, I still thought Riske was just doing his job and he was very honest. Rossi was the watch commander and Ron Phillips was the first detective on the scene. He was the one who talked to the secretary to find out where O.J. was. But I didn't have any great feelings about either of them. In the case of calling him in Chicago, the real question was, What was the man's demeanor? What did he say? I just want to know why did we have to go through all of that testimony and wait until he was cross-examined to say, well, you know, there were differences here about what was said and what the reaction was.

"Yeah, I was under the impression that O.J. said, 'Oh, my God, what do you mean she's dead?' " notes Carrie. "Right there it is questionable. Different statements by the same person. There was a lot of contradiction in their testimony."

On February 24, Judge Lance Ito and prosecutor Christopher Darden engage in a bitter exchange that results in Darden being cited for contempt of court in the first

victims' time of death based on the barking of Nicole's dog, which alerted neighbors and helped them discover the bodies of Simpson and Goldman.
• The jury takes a field trip to Nicole's condo and

*of a series of clashes between the judge and both teams
of attorneys.*

When all that happened between Chris Darden and the judge—
when he cited him for contempt of court—that's when we saw the
personalities really come out. We were surprised at that, at the
tone of it.

"I was just sitting there going, 'Damn,' " says Marsha.

Carrie adds, "I remember thinking it was no longer a witness
case. It was an attorney case. I was flabbergasted. But it wasn't the
only time. They did it all the way. Like when Marcia Clark got up
to talk about Johnnie Cochran's opening statement, the first thing
she said was, 'My pin is not as expensive as his pin. We do not
have the expensive lawyers.' And she just went on about how
much difference there was between them."

"Like it was competition," agrees Marsha.

"Right," Carrie continues. "And Johnnie Cochran's statement
was, 'They got all of California behind them. They can call anybody in here they want.' So, at that point, I'm seeing them at each
other right off the bat. So down the road seeing them do that little
nit-picking they were doing was expected. And it happened all the
way through the trial."

We all remember when we were getting selected, Cochran and
Shapiro went up to the podium together, arm in arm, saying,
"Well, we agree on the jury." Like they were on TV. They were
showboating. I don't think anyone appreciated that at all. I really
don't. I didn't appreciate the jokes. The glamour. To me, there was
no glamour at all in what was going on. They would sit there and

O.J. Simpson's estate. • **Week of February 13th** •
Prosecutor Marcia Clark unveils a dark knit cap and
a leather glove, which she claims were worn by
Simpson the night of the murders. • **Week of**

start laughing. I'm thinking, *What is so damned funny here?* There were floor shows so many times.

When it came to showboating, it was mostly on the defense's part. On the prosecution side, Marcia would just get too frustrated. I'm sitting right in front of her and I'm watching all her sighs and that to me was a sign of weakness. You're here to do a job and if something is bothering you, don't let them see you sweat. And Darden, too. You know, I wouldn't know what was happening when we weren't there, but he would be doing his jingle thing with his keys and his legs jiggled when things got tense. It made me think, *Well, if your case is so strong, why are you so frustrated?*

There was a lot of psychology being used by the defense team. Johnnie Cochran is a cocky bastard and he thought Marcia and Darden were not in his league. Darden and Cochran seemed like they had a little personal war going. It was all there. Marcia and Scheck, they always had their differences over evidence. And they would be snatching papers from each other. One would always complain that the other hadn't offered copies of paperwork or evidence. Cochran seemed to think it was funny that Marcia often showed signs of stress and frustration. I felt that Cochran thought he was really getting to her at times and that he liked it.

I had no information about the defense being called the "Dream Team." I could only say that the prosecution believed that they had a strong case but they were showing signs of stress and frustration. A lot of times Marcia would sigh and make gestures with her hands as though she were throwing in the towel. That didn't help her.

February 20th • Los Angeles police detective Tom Lange returns to witness stand. • Judge Lance Ito and Christopher Darden exchange words and the judge cites Darden for contempt of court. • Alibi

"I had absolutely no evidence that would point me in any other direction."

—Detective Tom Lange testifying on March 6 that authorities never considered anyone other than O.J. Simpson as a suspect in the murders.

In the middle of February we began what became over a month of testimony from detectives of the L.A.P.D.

By the time Lange came on the stand, we had heard from some of the establishing witnesses, Sukru Boztepe, Pablo Fenjves, those folks. We're starting to get into the case. To me, you're just laying things down. You get the guy who found the dog, and you're trying to put together what happened and when.

I felt that Lange did a pretty good job, based on his position. I guess he and Detective Phil Vannatter were partners, and I sort of felt Lange should have done a good job. I guess he would have been the one who was more experienced, but I felt he didn't use his experience to more or less dominate the situation the way he should have. He tried to be equal with Vannatter, and there was nothing equal about them at all.

"Right. I'm just gathering at this point," says Marsha. "I'm trying to get the times down. The dog wailing, the dog being in the street, what happened when Riske showed up, and then what happened when they went over to notify O.J."

"I was thinking about all four of those deputies going over to Rockingham as opposed to taking care of the business at Bundy," remarks Carrie. "A lot of the evidence deteriorated. They had a lot of time to get O.J.. Even if he went to another country, as well

---

witness Rosa Lopez testifies in a special hearing without jury present. • **Week of February 27th** • A fourth (male) juror is dismissed with no public explanation given. • Rosa Lopez repeatedly

known as he was, they were going to find O.J.. It's like, we want you right now. That's the way it appeared to me."

It seemed the police spent all of this time trying to cover up the fact that Mr. Simpson was not a suspect and how they originally went over there because they had just been to a double homicide and they wanted to make sure nothing was going on at Rockingham. Once they gave this news to Mr. Simpson, if he became distraught, then they could go and take him over to see about the children. The information about them thinking that something may have gone on inside the Rockingham home was one thing, but why did they send Arnelle to the door first? To me, that was amazing.

I mean, you go into the house. You spotted blood there prior to going into the house. So you scaled the wall and now you get into the backyard and get Arnelle to let you into the house. No one ever goes upstairs. No one ever searches the house. You're walking around here. You've got no protection. Your guns aren't drawn. If you really thought someone was on the premises, what's up on this? Remember, too, that time in the '89 incident when she ran out of the house and she had mentioned to the police that he had guns in the house, and they were just casually walking around, just letting him go back in the house and then come out, get in the car, and drive off. Never arrested him. It doesn't make sense.

But everyone can be confused or make a mistake—that's human nature. Honesty would have played a great part. If they had said, "We knew they had problems before, we just wanted to check," that would make sense. They would already know about

---

contradicts herself and answers "I don't know" to many questions during her appearance on the stand. • **Week of March 6th** • Detective Tom Lange tells the court that he did not consider anyone other

past incidents. I could understand wanting to follow up, but this bull corn about telling stories and getting the judge to believe there was so much blood out there, you felt you had to go over there and check it because you thought O.J. might have been a victim himself. That was a bunch of baloney.

I think it might have been reasonable to suspect Mr. Simpson, based on the past history he had, but they weren't straight with us about why they chose to do what they did, and that made us suspect everything else we heard from them. That's the thing with Vannatter when he was saying O.J. was not the prime suspect. Why would he even get up there with that lie? Why didn't he just tell the truth? Don't tell me you're going to go to the house because you think maybe the same thing is happening over on Rockingham and you're concerned about the Rockingham family. And then the first person you send in the door is the daughter. If you're so concerned, you're the police, why don't you walk through the door with your guns drawn saying whatever the spiel is you give. Search and seize or whatever the situation. But the information or whatever the testimony was that Arnelle walked through first really did not wash. And in the meantime, you had gone over there and wasted all this time and everything has degraded and the bodies have decomposed to a point where you can't even get the liver test done. The coroner is not called in. No one followed any procedures that the police normally follow. To me, they seemed so wrapped up in trying to catch someone that they forgot that it took evidence to get him. And everybody's over there at Rockingham. That wasn't the crime scene. No one is working over at Bundy. The bodies are still there at Bundy. No one's there.

than O.J. Simpson as a suspect. • Detective Mark Fuhrman takes the stand. • **Week of March 13th** • Mark Fuhrman is grilled by defense attorney F. Lee Bailey. Fuhrman remains calm and cool and stands

So, from jump street I'm very, very concerned why you would neglect what you're supposed to do to try to solve a crime, which is gather and protect the evidence.

So, right from the start, the bodies are out there, all the evidence is lying out there, and the police are running over to Rockingham to notify O.J. that his ex-wife was murdered. I didn't understand that, especially when they have Fuhrman, their lead man who has this racial problem, doing all the spearheading. You've got Fuhrman searching and finding the glove and going places and finding the stain. It was dark and he finds little lines on a vehicle with a penlight. To me that's unusual unless he has superhuman vision or something. Then after he gets there, why doesn't he go upstairs if he is really thinking this man is dead? Why isn't he looking for this? Then when he knows that Mr. Simpson is all right, he stays there. Ten hours over there at Rockingham while the bodies and everything else degrade. Why didn't he go back to the scene? He could have always gotten in touch with O.J. if that's who he was really looking for but there he is so busy trying to nail this right here that he lets everything else go to pot. This is very important.

When the police were testifying there always seemed to be controversy over whatever they said or did. Anytime the L.A.P.D. took the witness stand, they always had to come back again and reiterate. Case in point, Vannatter and the Fiato brothers and the issue of talking about the case. I mean, just say straight out, "Yes, we talked about the case. It wasn't anything intentional. It was just something that happened to come up. The whole world was talking about the case." And, "Yeah, I may have said he was a suspect

by his original account of his actions on the night of the murders. • Fuhrman is questioned again; this time the questions are pointedly focused on racial slurs that were reportedly overheard and asserts

because the husband is always a suspect." Just be straight out instead of going back and forth. It was really no big deal, but the police made it a big deal, just trying to make themselves look good, and that's where they ran into problems.

"All they had to say was, 'I made a mistake.' We can understand that," Marsha says.

"He had all the time in the world to correct his statement," Carrie adds. "When they called him back the last time, Vannatter had plenty of time to say, 'Well, I might have said something to them while we were having a beer. I was off-duty.' But he sat there again under oath and said, 'No, I never said that.' Then here come the Fiato brothers and, bam, the FBI."

And then he was running around town with the blood vial rather than booking it in properly. Just be straight out and say you did it, say, "I made a mistake. Through the excitement of this case, I just got wrapped up and made a mistake." We are human. We can understand these human errors. But when you sit up there and lie about it is when you have problems.

As Carrie points out, "Vannatter said the reason he had the blood vial and brought it to Rockingham was due to the fact that he did not have a booking number and he wanted to book all the evidence at the same time. Well, let me ask you this. Who would be the better person to get the booking number than the head investigator or the detectives? Even if he just went in there and booked that one thing, he would have had a booking number to bring back to Fung, who kept all the stuff overnight. Everything. He didn't book anything. Matter of fact, he didn't book the blood for three days."

that the bloody glove was planted because Fuhrman is a racist. • A fifth male juror is removed, reportedly for working on a book about the case. • **Week of March 20th** • Brian "Kato" Kaelin testifies

"And I think Lange was trying to cover up, too," Marsha says. "I think Vannatter messed up. I truly did not believe about him not being able to go and get the blood booked in. That he carried that blood around didn't work with me at all and then giving it to Fung and him not telling Mazzola. It was an important piece of evidence. I considered it one of the most important pieces of evidence. It was mishandled. As far as his testimony, I just feel he was trying to cover his own ass. I don't think he was in cahoots with anybody, but I think he was trying to cover his ass. I think it was sloppiness. I don't think it was a conspiracy at all. I think it started out bad so they immediately started covering up some of this stuff. I truly think Vannatter and Fuhrman knew they messed up somewhere over at Bundy. They were trying to get the collar. They started walking around the house. I don't put it past Fuhrman picking up all that stuff out there. I don't put it past him. I don't put it past Vannatter trying to help him. They just botched up, messed up, and when they tried to cover up for themselves, it just got out of control."

"You say under oath that you have not addressed any black person as a 'nigger' or spoken about black people as 'niggers' in the past ten years, Detective Fuhrman?" asks F. Lee Bailey on March 15.
"That's what I'm saying, sir," responds Fuhrman.

After hearing the testimony of Officer Riske, Sergeant Rossi, and Detectives Phillips and Lange, Mark Fuhrman walked to the

to hearing a loud thump outside his guest house on the night of the murders. • Kaelin testifies that Simpson had encouraged him to say that he was in his house at 9:40 P.M. on the night of the murders,

witness stand. A moment later, my mind told me that he was a snake. I just sort of knew that he was a snake. Matter of fact, I think in my journal I indicated that my first feeling when I saw him, he sort of looked like a Ku Klux Klan or a skinhead with hair, that type of thing. He was too clean-cut and too calm, too cool. The way he walked in, it was as if to say, "I'm it. I know who I am." And when he testified, he had this sternness about him. The defense tried to discredit him, but I have to say that I felt that what he had found at Rockingham did not look good for O.J., because Fuhrman was good and stern in his testimony.

Then, when I found out through later testimony that he had had witness training, if I had been allowed to raise my hand, I would have asked, "Why would it be necessary for an officer with his experience to have any type of witness training?" This is not the first time he's been to court. After the information came out about the young real estate lady, Kathleen Bell, who wrote the letter about things he had said to her, things she had heard him say, it didn't make me feel any better about him. When he was being examined by the prosecution, he was cool, calm, and collected. But when the defense started to interview him, his whole demeanor changed. His breathing patterns shifted and, from where I was sitting, you could see him squirming. You could see the tension in his hands. You see, I wanted to make eye-to-eye contact with every witness who went on that stand. I wanted you to look at me and tell me this is what you feel or think. Fuhrman kept pushing his feet up against the back board of the stand. You could tell there was just a little anger building up in him. I'm thinking, "This man is lying." You could see it right there. I

thereby providing Simpson with an alibi. • **Week of March 27th** • Allan Parks, the limousine driver who took Simpson to the airport on the night of the murders, testifies that the white Bronco had not

thought I was the only one who saw it until we got into the deliberation room and I found that other people saw it, too.

When Fuhrman came in, they couldn't discredit him or say anything until he started lying. I didn't have a problem with his earlier testimony, but I disbelieved Fuhrman when he actually said he didn't use the word *nigger*. I believed that he was lying then. I hadn't even heard the tapes then. You could tell he used the word *nigger*. You could look at Fuhrman, just the way he said, "No. Never," and know he wasn't being straight. As soon as he said no, I thought, "Oh, come on. Sure you have." The one lie that he should have just never said was when they were asking him, "Have you ever used the n-word?" He should have come right out and said, "Of course, I've used the n-word. Tell me who doesn't use the n-word out there dealing with these people?" He would have been a lot better off.

When I heard those things about the n-word, it was like a hot flash hit me. It just made me realize how badly I hate that word. For him to sit up here and pretend that he never used it, it made me feel like just jumping up and slapping him down right then and there.

"Detective Vannatter, did you rush to judgment in this case?" prosecutor Christopher Darden asks on March 20.

"No," Vannatter replies.

If Fuhrman wasn't damaging enough, we then had Detective Vannatter. With twenty-seven years of experience on the force, I could

been parked at the Simpson house. He also relates that a male figure entered the house at 10:56 P.M., followed by the lights coming on and Simpson finally appearing. •

not understand how he could allow himself to ride around with Mr. Simpson's blood vial in the car. Experience itself should have told him that this is not a good thing to do. I couldn't understand why he would allow himself to discuss the case with others like the Fiato brothers. What happened to confidentiality? And then there's the fact that he indicated that Mr. Simpson was not a suspect when everybody knows if there's a husband or an ex-husband around Nicole, he will be a suspect until proven otherwise. So, just say that. It's not necessary to lie and say the man was not a suspect. Common sense can tell you that, yes, he was, of course you'd suspect someone in that position. So I sort of lost respect for him then and it continued down the line.

"Vannatter never looked at the jury. Vannatter didn't do no looking. Vannatter always stared out straight ahead and he had a redness that came to his face when you were getting next to him," says Carrie. "You're looking at all these people. You're waiting. You can watch their mannerisms, their expressions. You got eye-to-eye contact. You're waiting for them to tell you and look at you. I'm not going to say Vannatter is not a good detective. But he got up there and stated he had never spoken about the O.J. Simpson case to anybody, and the next thing you know, we're hearing from those brothers. Then the FBI came up and pulled the cover off of him. I thought that was bad.

"And Vannatter was the one who handled the blood," Carrie continues. "Vannatter was the one Fuhrman spoke to about what he was doing around the house and wound up contradicting himself because Fuhrman said he did not tell Vannatter. That was a lie right there between the two of them. These are the things we

Week of April 3rd • Criminalist Dennis Fung details the methodology used to gather blood samples at the murder site. • Fung presents photos of bloodstains on Simpson's Bronco. He concedes

listened to. Then Vannatter got a little emotional when the defense asked him, 'Oh, you do what Fuhrman says?' 'No, I don't have to do what Fuhrman says. Fuhrman can't tell me what to do.' That made him very emotional on that witness stand. It was a contradiction."

Carrie went on. "Then he said, 'Well, I was standing up front.' 'Well, where are the notes to say what happened?' 'I didn't do any notes,' he says. 'Lange wrote all the notes.' You know Vannatter didn't do any writing. Lange did all the writing between them. You should have had your notes for what you did, not have someone do them for you. But, then, that's my opinion. So, when it came down to listening about Fuhrman and the various things that went down, Lange wasn't left out. Even though those shoes they first took as evidence may not have been the shoes worn for the murders, why put them under your arm, lay them around, and get trace evidence? Why didn't you just slip the shoes in a plastic bag so whatever was on them could have been protected?

"I think it was a rush to judgment, but the reason I say it was a rush to judgment is because in the first place the deputies left the bodies when they should have stayed on the scene," Carrie emphasizes. "That's rush. Second, you do all this work within a matter of three days, that's still a rush. Three to four days. And, no matter what they say, he was a prime suspect. He was a suspect from jump street. I'm talking the rushing to judgment is to rush and just go right after O.J. as opposed to doing what you are supposed to do. That's rush. O.J. would have been around. You would have found him with a beard on or not."

that a trainee gathered most of the critical blood samples. • A sixth juror is removed for failing to reveal a history of spousal abuse. • Judge Ito denies a defense request for a hearing on the admissibility

"You consider yourself to be the defendant's friend, don't you, Mr. Kaelin?" asks prosecutor Marcia Clark on March 22.

"Yes. I'm still a friend. I'm . . . I know my job is to be 100 percent honest and that's what I'm going to do," he replies.

For most of us Kato seemed like a young man who was just out there trying to make it, but I must admit the first thing I thought when he came to the witness stand is he must be a drug dealer because he looked like he was high and he had that confused look about him while he was on the stand. I don't know what anybody else thought about him, but that was my personal feeling. Kato was as honest as he could be to a degree, not knowing whether what he said was going to be crucial or not.

I thought that he was trying to be careful in a lot of things he said. That was my first impression, because I felt he was trying to protect his environment. You know, the man's living rent-free, eating and partying, and doing his thing for little or nothing and he had the best of both worlds. He really doesn't want to put himself out of there. But what really got me was when he said he was offered $1 million for his story and he had not sold it. And, I'm thinking to myself, *Is this man a fool?* Who's he trying to fool? He's a starving artist, an actor, and you tell me that you finally hit the gold mine, the million-dollar goldmine, and you're not going to take it? We weren't born yesterday. And I figured he was just mainly trying to cover up a lot. Basically, he didn't want to put himself in a predicament where he wouldn't have any place to stay

of DNA evidence. • **Week of April 10th** • Judge Ito subpoenas dismissed juror Jeanette Harris. • After five days hiatus, testimony resumes with Dennis Fung. • **Week of April 17th** • Fung finishes

when this man got out, depending on how his life was set up after he got out.

Still, I felt that he did not give us his true opinion. Or maybe it was just that the prosecution did not ask the right questions. He may have been holding back something. He made me feel that way. I said, "Okay, he's an actor. And actors spend the majority of their time memorizing things, scripts and stuff." And then all of a sudden he couldn't remember certain things. I thought at that point, *We got an actor here. They spend the majority of their life remembering things.* I felt he was holding back. I also felt Marcia probably pushed just a little bit too hard on him. She just totally degraded him right down and she pushed him just a little hard. If she eased up just a little bit maybe he would have broken through. He held on, but I felt—I shouldn't say that I could see—I felt that he was high the couple of days that he was on the stand.

"Kato Kaelin came to court just as high as he wanted to be. I think he was on some type of speed. That's the impression he gave me," adds Marsha. "He was trying to be as much a help to O.J. as possible, but he didn't know how to go about doing it. Sometimes he acted like he didn't know how they were putting the questions. I'm not saying he was lying. I'm just saying he was trying to tell the truth the best he knew how. But he was high as hell. I truly believe he was high. Smacking his lips—I know that from just being exposed to people who are high. And I thought he was trying to work around not giving any type of incriminating evidence. I didn't think he really wanted to be there, first off. I think he was trying to be careful in how he answered the questions. Kind of

testimony, admitting that some procedural errors were made in gathering the blood samples, but none that would have had serious consequences. • Judge Ito questions the jury about possible racial

work around the answers. He didn't volunteer information. But I believe he knew more than he let on."

> *On March 29, limousine driver Allan Parks reiterates his earlier testimony that when he scanned the curb for the house number at 10:22 P.M., he did not see the Bronco parked in front of the Rockingham residence, nor did he see it seventeen minutes later when he went around to another entrance.*

I don't care what anyone says but I thought Allan Parks was honest in his testimony. He was excited about picking up O.J. Simpson. That was his main thing, as was getting him to the airport on time. The question came up about him seeing the Bronco parked on Rockingham. I thought that if he was not looking for a car—because basically all he was looking for was a better way to enter into the property—then he would not have seen it. He was being as honest as he possibly could. I also felt that the young man who checked the luggage in for Mr. Simpson just reported what he did. He was honest in that.

> *On April 5, criminalist Dennis Fung concedes that investigators made mistakes at the murder scene that had possibly contaminated some crucial physical evidence in the case. "I would prefer that it was not done," Fung tells defense attorney Barry Scheck.*

tensions and other problems within the jury. • **Week of April 24th** • Thirteen jurors dress in black and refuse to continue the trial until Judge Ito meets with them to discuss problems. • **Week of May 1st** •

Foreman Armanda Cooley, Marsha Rubin-Jackson, and Carrie Bess
(From left to right)

Armanda Cooley

7/24/95

Quet ETA found
on socks & gate
are in parts
per million

Questions regarding
the mass amount
being parts per
million instead of
parts per billion as
indicated in the
articles the
witness relied upon to
provide his testimony

Testimony regarding
Agus March testing
his own blood &
found approx. the
same amt EDTA
located on gate &
sock

July 24, 1995
Testimony of Dr. Fredric Rieders

4/6/95   Direct

Dr. Lakshmanan

Q. The clothes were
re-examined in
March 1995 - additional
defects (3) were located
on the Goldman shirt
& pants

Discussed ERRORS
(Brett Eden)
in labeling & no
mention of scraping
envelope, these
errors were the
responsibility of DR
Golden   also fail to address
the contusion found
on Nicole's brain & several dictating
mistakes

June 6, 1995
Testimony of Dr. Lakshamanan Sathyavagiswaran

4/5/95   Fung

Location of poss. blood staining
no fibers or staining located
in walkway between
swing gate & location
of gloves.

re: Possible contamination of the
Bundy crime scene
from the blanket used
to cover a female victim
from secondary transfer. Trace
evidence.

admonition
① Do not discuss the case
② Do not allow any one to
talk to you about the case
③ Do not form any opinion about the
case.
④ Do not deliberate the case
before it has been assigned
to go

April 5, 1995
Testimony of Dennis Fung

Presentation of County of Los Angeles 1990 Employee of the Year Commendation to Armanda Cooley by Peter Schabarum, County Supervisor, 1st District, Los Angeles County

Armanda Cooley's daughter, Yolanda

Armanda Cooley in front of Room 530, her 267-day residence at the Hotel Inter-Continental in Downtown Los Angeles

Carrie Bess

ON SITE - 2/12/95
ARRIVED AT RON's 11660 - HOME
9:58 - 9:59 MEZZALUNA -
APPROX. 2/3 min. LEFT REST.
10:00 3/4 min.

DOROTHY -- 11900

121
900 Bundy

898 Yell? who lives Ktape
Front of 875
Possible to see from st. About 15/20
ft.
Came to get visual. House was
blocked by bushes.

Blood could have ran out onto side
walk.
Gate was possible to see.

Gate where RON was found
Area - Bushes hard for too people
to stand in a fight without the other
person getting hurt.

February 12, 1995
Jury visitation to crime scene and related
site visits

GARY SIMS. REDIRECT. 5/22/65
1/2/95 - Long time to 24
WORK Sept 8, 17 - 4 (1) - 20 - 14
15 - 16 - 17 - 18 - 19 - 20 - 26 - 293 - 305
29 30 31 32 34 55 293 - 305 -
with DR. DRAKE there 2/3 Times AS
Long (273).

GLOVE #9 Rock. Sun.
Sub - Field mix -
''   IN LAB
''   IN LAB CARRYOVER
IN Control - dots -
          MIXTURE
BRONCO 31 - 304 - 305
- 275 A - RT
(18) All There Are time when
Some Are the same. 275B -
OI R N B   (C) b48-5047
24   8 ?   OJ L N R B B
275D   30   305   B = = = = = =
       BSR N B
       = = = =
                          Cont. 5/31/95

MR.
Larry Fiato   Defence   9/19/95
How Long Know VanAtter
3/4 Time. Conversation)
He did State he went over
there with OJ as a suspect
Feb.

CROSS   9/19/95
He said he went
to OJ's House because
he was a suspect.

May 22, 1995
Testimony of Gary Sims

September 19, 1995
Testimony of Larry Fiato

Carrie Bess with her brother, James William Smith, at Washington High School class reunion in Caruthersville, Missouri

Cousin Harold Thomas and his wife Tamara

Carrie Bess *(left)* and her sister Lula Ann Lewis

Carrie Bess in front of Room 517, her 267-day residence at the Hotel Inter-Continental in Downtown Los Angeles

15 MARCH 95   MARK FUHRMAN

NO MEMORY OF SIMULATED GRAND JURY QUESTIONS
THAT TOOK PLACE 4-6 WKS AGO. (DIOSS) RELIGHT
FLASHLIGHT - UPGRADED BEING RELIEVED BY RHD PUT
BLUE BLAZER IN CAR - (DIOSS) WALKWAY TO 875 -
(DIOST) PHOTO OF AREA WHERE GLOVE ÷ CAP FOUND AT 875 -
QUESTIONED NO NEIGHBORS AT ROCKINGHAM- DID NOT
RECORD NORTHSIDE NEIGHBORS OF ROCKINGHAM NAME -
NEVER UPON ENTERING HOME ASKED WHERE OJ WAS

16 MARCH 95
NORA VICTOR NORA (NVN) - NEVER USED TO TALK TO
OTHER DETECTIVES OVER RADIO · DOESN'T EVER
REMEMBER USING THE TERM "NIGGER" WHEN REFERRING
TO BLACKS

March 15 and 16, 1995
Testimony of Mark Fuhrman

---

10 AUGUST 1995

DR. MICHAEL BADEN:
BY HANDS NOT BEING WRAPPED COULD HAVE LOST
EVIDENCE - MEDICAL EXAMINERS EXAMINATION
OF HOME AND CONTENTS VITAL TO INVESTIGATION -
"RAPE KIT" NECESSARY ON MURDERED WOMEN -
STOMACH CONTENTS OF RONALD SHOWS HE ATE
RAISINS AFTER PASTA - NOT RECORDED BY
MEDICAL DOCTOR GOLDEN - ALSO NOT RECORDED
"KALE, CELERY TOMATO" - RIGATONI EATEN BY NICOLE
AFTER LEAVING RESTAURANT - M.E. (MEDICAL EXAM)
CAN'T TELL HOW MANY ASSAILANTS, DOUBLE OR
SINGLE EDGED KNIFE (USED) - ALSO UNKNOWN
TO HEIGHT WEIGHT BUILD OF "KILLER(S)" -
HARD TO DETERMINE BRUISES BY PHOTOS (IF
BEFORE DEATH OR AFTER (CUTS ALSO) -
    NOTE: NICOLE HAD ACRYLIC NAILS
          HARD TO SCRATCH AND MAKE A SCAR
          OR DRAW BLOOD
OPINION IS NICOLE RECEIVED STAB ÷ FATAL WOUNDS
WHILE ~~struck~~ ALERT -
NO EVIDENCE OF SHOE PRINT ON NICOLES CLOTHING
OR BACK - STRUGGLE BTWN NICOLE ÷ ASSAILANT
ENSUED - STAB WOUNDS (CLUSTER) ON NECK
KNIFE ENTERED FROM DIFFERENT DIRECTION

August 10, 1995
Testimony of Dr. Michael Baden

---

7 AUGUST 1995
DR. JOHN GERDES:
P573) DQ ALPHA TYPING SHEET DATED 10/16/94
P574) DQ ALPHA TYPING SHEET   10/31/94

P575) HYBRIDIZATION (DNA) SHEET(S)
D1315A) HYBRIDIZATION 4/4 LINES BLOCKED OUT
D 1315 B)   "   4 LINES READABLE

August 7, 1995
Testimony of Dr. John Gerdes

Marsha Rubin-Jackson and husband Danny Jackson on their wedding day, March 31, 1994

Son Kevin Brown, 19 years old

Marsha's sister Linda Rubin, niece Jordan Hine, nephew Jonathan Rubin-King, and mother Maxine Rubin

Grandson Kevin, Jr., born September 29, 1994

Marsha Rubin-Jackson in front of Room 525, her 267-day residence at the Hotel Inter-Continental in Downtown Los Angeles

An interior view of a typical juror room at the Hotel Inter-Continental

Hotel room smoke detector and fire alarm units thought by jurors to house audio and video monitors

Some of the most exciting testimony was between Barry Scheck and Dennis Fung. I felt that Dennis was too busy trying to be protective of his position. His rank is a Criminalist II, but somewhere along the line I think he missed something. I think that he did not do a professional job in collecting the evidence. The whole thing about putting that evidence in the truck with no refrigerator was ridiculous. Mazzola was young and new on the job. Mazzola was sitting there in the living room and nodded out for twenty minutes or so. If she didn't have anything to do for nearly a half hour, she could have taken the evidence to Parker Center or wherever, and had it booked or refrigerated while Dennis continued to collect or do whatever he had to do. I think what happened is a lot of people just got too caught up in the moment and didn't do their jobs properly. I just thought he was sloppy. If there was any type of conspiracy that he was more or less involved in, I thought it was just trying to correct some of the things he may have done wrong to start with, such as documenting the evidence properly, rather than trying to frame anybody.

"Please remember my admonition to you: Do not discuss the case among yourselves. Don't form any opinions about the case. Don't conduct any deliberations until the matter has been submitted to you. Do not allow anyone to communicate with you in regards to the case."

—Admonition of Judge Lance Ito every time the jury
recessed from court

Judge Ito removes a seventh juror at her own request. • **Week of May 8th** • A biochemist presents the genetic match of blood samples at the murder scene and the blood of O.J. Simpson,

I think in terms of where the jury lost patience with Judge Ito is that we felt the trial was just going on too long. You had situations where there were certain witnesses that came back two or three times saying the same thing. For instance, Rubin, the expert on the Aris Isotoner Extra Light Gloves, he was there three times. It was totally ridiculous. And the last time he just ruined himself by showing that he was biased to the prosecution, saying "I'll see you at the victory party" or something like that, which was totally stupid. But those are the types of things that happen when you constantly allow repeated action.

I think this trial went on entirely too long. Under no condition should they ever allow this to happen again. Whatever happens, if you're going to do your discovery and have your hearings, have all that stuff at the beginning before the jury is even selected, then have the trial. I don't know how many actual days we were in court, the actual amount of time. But I'm sure that it could have all been completed in three months. I know a person's life is on the line. I know it should not be rushed because of that, but I still don't think it should take that long. I think we need to look at the judicial system in that respect. Judge Ito's main thing was, whatever the lawyers are doing out there is just show. I want your full attention on this witness stand. And that's basically what I tried to do, center myself on this witness stand.

I respect Judge Ito. I like him. You just had that feeling that you could talk to him. I have no reason to state that anything he said he would try to do, he did not do. He left it open for us to talk to him, to communicate with him about anything. I really

linking Simpson to the murder scene. He claims the odds are 1 in 170 million that someone other than Simpson could have left the bloodstains at the murder scene. • **Week of May 15th** • DNA expert

have no quarrel with Judge Ito even though I was bored stiff with a lot of that repetitious stuff. But it wasn't for me to call the shots.

I also thought that the deputies were unjustly removed by the judge. We told the sergeant that we were not going to work until we talked to him. Judge Ito called us in one by one. Everybody voiced his or her opinion on how these deputies were dismissed and that at no time had they exhibited any type of racism toward us. We thought it was unfair that he did what he did. We told him and he listened.

"Judge Ito . . . he read that admonition to us every day," recalls Carrie. "Once I learned it, I would say it along with him—just mouth it—and he looked at me once or twice, really looked at me, like, 'Stop it!' "

In the closing minutes of testimony on Tuesday, May 9, jurors see DNA samples from O.J. Simpson and the two murder victims for the first time. Expert testimony over DNA evidence and blood found at the scene of the crime and in O.J. Simpson's Bronco, his socks, and the gloves found at Bundy and Rockingham would last more than a month.

After we got out, we heard about others watching the DNA testimony on TV and how difficult it was to keep track of the details. Our sentiments exactly. Witness after witness, day after day. Of all witnesses, Robin Cotton was excellent. The lady knows her job.

Gary Sims testifies that the blood on the glove found at Simpson's house matches the blood of Ronald Goldman. • **Week of May 22nd** • Judge Ito removes the eighth juror from the trial. No reason is

She's highly professional. But I think she put a little too much emphasis on her exhibits and on trying to relay information to us. What happened is, she lost us, and I say us because I believe that everybody felt the same way. She talked down and when you talk down to people, you tend to lose them. They feel that, well, she thinks you don't understand anyway, so why should I spend a lot of time and effort listening to what she says? When we went on break and walked into the deliberation room, everybody heaved a sigh of relief.

She talked down to us like we were illiterates," says Marsha. "I didn't like that, but the woman knew what she was talking about."

"There's no doubt in my mind that Robin Cotton proved and tested what they sent her, but that did not mean it wasn't cross-contaminated before it got there," adds Carrie.

I agree with Marsha. I felt that she talked down to us because she felt that the mentality of the jury was not at her level. When I got out, I kept hearing more and more people saying there was only one graduate on the jury and so forth, so that indicates to me that they felt everybody else was illiterate. Maybe the first people who got out there and started talking and interviewing with the press gave that impression. But there were some very intelligent people on that jury panel. They should be commended for that. The boredom came in when people treated you as if you were a kindergartner or first grader. I realize that if you have a Ph.D. and you're talking to someone who does not have training in the field of serology or forensic science, you might assume they're not going to understand some of the basics. Of course, you're not going to understand the total details of that field, but you don't

given for the removal. • **Week of May 29th** • Due to Judge Ito's ruling, prosecutors are prevented from presenting evidence of carpet fibers from Simpson's Bronco that were found at the murder

have to. Unfortunately, there's no way to let the people know that you got it. You can't just raise your hand and say, "Dr. Cotton, I understand what you're talking about. Move on."

I thought Gary Sims, from the California Department of Justice, was an outstanding witness, too. He's professional. He knows his job. Matter of fact, it was through him that I started to learn a little bit more about the DNA processing because he spoke to us at our level. Between him and Barry Scheck is how we were able to pick up a lot about the DNA process. And Renee Montgomery, same difference. I mean, these people did an outstanding job. Cellmark, D.O.J., even the FBI. They did an outstanding job with their testing facility. The testing facilities seemed to be top of the line and this is the impression that I received. But you can only test what you receive.

Collin Yamauchi, however, was too busy trying to protect his department, justifying the errors that were made and trying to make corrections. It was the same with all of the L.A.P.D. right from the start; no one wanted to say, "Hey, we made a mistake." That stands in contrast to Dr. Lakshamanan—he was one of my favorite witnesses. A very personable man. I enjoyed him simply because he was just the opposite from the L.A.P.D. He was protective of his department, but he still verified all the errors that were made by his department.

"It was like with Fung and Mazzola," says Carrie. "I just cannot believe they didn't have the proper training. I think they just got caught up and were in a rush and just mishandled things. They just got caught mishandling stuff and then tried to cover it up with explanations that never added up."

site. Prosecutors failed to notify the defense of the new evidence before June 1, as required. • **Week of June 5th** • Judge Ito removes two more jurors, the ninth and tenth, bringing the number of available

"Their techniques just started getting sloppy, the way they handled the evidence," says Marsha. "And that Mazzola, she was just trying to cover her ass. Mishandled the evidence. Misnumbered it. Mislabeled it."

"Mazzola was really trying to cover for Fung, you could see that," continues Carrie. "He'd say he did something and she knew she'd done it. She collected stuff and he said he collected it. It was a pretty bad situation. And there are probably a lot of other people who couldn't afford attorneys to come in and question their ability. God knows how many people are in jail right now due to their negligence."

When you're in a situation where you're trying to do more with less, these are the types of things that happen. You get sloppy work. It's impossible to believe that this is the first case that they had thirty or forty errors on. This is the first one where they may have gotten caught. If they had this amount of errors on this particular case, they've had errors on other cases because they're rushing through the process and not taking the necessary time to do the job properly. When you are working with homicides and with the prosecution, you need this information to be as valid as possible. I think it is high time that the department look into updating their procedures and taking time to do the job properly.

It was the same story over and over when it came to how evidence was collected and stored. I had a hard time with Mr. Peratis. His first testimony as a witness was okay. But when he had to go back again and indicate he's not sure about how much blood he drew, I had a problem because he's been a nurse for what, twenty, thirty years? He draws blood all the time. I figured if you're doing

alternates down to two. The woman is removed for warning another juror about an investigation of her book deal, while the male juror is dropped for allegedly "intimidating" other jurors. • The coroner

this on a consistent basis, I have a problem when you state you don't know how much you draw. Because his testimony in the first place was, "Yes, I did draw 8 cc's. It could have been 7.9 or 8.1 because this is something I do all the time. I would have been either under 1 cc or over 1 cc." But, then all of a sudden, the new testimony is he doesn't know, the syringe was turned a different way and it was a 10-cc syringe instead of an 8-cc syringe. I had a real problem with that.

I also had a problem with Michele Kestler from the L.A.P.D. crime lab. Because of her position, I felt she should have had a little more to say. Her total testimony was, "I don't remember. Yes, I was there at the meeting. I don't know who was there. I didn't take notes." I know when I attend meetings—and I'm not near at the level that she's in—somebody is at that meeting who will take notes and you will get copies of those notes. They don't have to be great notes, just basically who was present and what the meeting was pertaining to. I had a real problem with somebody at her level not knowing or forgetting or "I didn't have anything to do with this." Because at your level, you are responsible for what anybody and everybody does who is under you. So you have to be a little more aggressive about taking responsibility.

Like Dr. Henry Lee. Now he was a very impressive gentleman. Highly intelligent, world-renowned. I had a lot of respect for Dr. Lee. There's just something about his approach that makes you respect him. And maybe it's because of his professional background. I sort of felt that the prosecution dogged him out basically when he was trying to test some of the items and they wouldn't give him either the proper equipment or the time neces-

describes his scenario of how the attack on the two victims took place, complete with autopsy photos.
• **Week of June 12th** • The coroner demonstrates on his own body where stab wounds were received

sary to investigate like he wanted to. But, basically, I liked him. He was a very impressive witness.

On the whole, I did not find DNA too complicated to grasp because Barry Scheck took time to explain it and we really observed and listened to what those people were telling us. Now, granted, we may not be experts in that field because we never studied DNA. I certainly didn't, but I was aware of what they were talking about. I understood that there's degrading of DNA. I understood the amount of blood that it took to really come up with a good reading. I understood when they talked about the autorads and the aliels. Day in and day out they talked about them. These **are** things I wanted to understand, the things I wanted to see. These spots that you filed, 48, 49, 50, 51, and 52. I wanted to see this. I wanted to see the EDTA that you talked about. I wanted to know these things. I listened to them. You really don't have to be a chemist or a scientist to be oriented to the front part of something, especially if you're told step by step and you go home and that's all you can see at night. Going through those autorads and those aliels and how they talk about degrading and how much blood it takes. I see us not being so naive on those points.

Basically there were no problems with the blood evidence. They tested it and not only did the L.A.P.D. test it, but the Department of Justice tested it, Cellmark tested it, the FBI did some testing, and they found what they found. And each agency was compatible with its findings. The only blood evidence that was in dispute as far as deliberation was concerned was the blood evidence found on the fence, which was no. 117.

by Nicole Simpson and Ron Goldman. An alternate juror leaves the courtroom in distress over the testimony. • O.J. Simpson struggles to put on the bloody gloves in open court. They do not appear to

That was blood they picked up, what, two weeks later, the end of June or something like that—June 26, or something like that. And the fact that it had not degraded and it had more DNA in it than most of the evidence they had collected, that was the problem that we had. And the other problem we had as far as the blood evidence was concerned was the blood found on the console of the Bronco weeks later.

My biggest problem was, there were .07 cc's of blood in the Bronco. Total. But you go back days, weeks later and get some more. Now, we don't know what could have happened between that time. Here's this vehicle down at the O.P.G. Anyone could have gone down there and got anything. We don't know what you got going. We don't know anything about the swatches, which were wet in certain places. You have to take all these things under consideration. Why were these swatches wet? If you say you put all these swatches in a drying area, we're looking at contamination for sure.

We're talking about mixing and commingling and dealing with things and working so rapidly. I'm not saying that it really happened or how it happened, but something went wrong. It went wrong to the point where they want everybody to ask, "Why was O.J.'s blood at Bundy?" Okay, maybe it was O.J.'s blood at Bundy. It was O.J.'s blood on the gate. All I could say after hearing all that was, well, maybe it was, but you let this blood degrade. You should have been there doing your job. Now you want to tell us that EDTA was on the blood at the gate. It should have deteriorated along with the other sample, especially two weeks later.

fit. • **Week of June 19th** • An FBI expert testifies that the person who killed Nicole and Ron wore expensive Italian shoes the same size that O.J. Simpson wears. •

EDTA is something that's found in all of us, but there's such a narrow margin. Because if it was that high, our blood wouldn't clot. So why didn't that deteriorate, too?

"They were looking to see how much EDTA was in there and in order to see it you have to have all of these ions in there for it to be present," Carrie explains. "And Herbert MacDonell stated that the ions were there, all of them. But the guy who tested the EDTA said it wasn't fair and all of the signs showed the same wavelength. When he was asked about it, about all the wavelengths being the same, he said that was just noise in the machine. That the machine was noisy. So the question we had was, How can you call this set 'noise' and tell us we should ignore it, even though it had the same frequencies as the one that represents the presence of the ions? So I think he picked the parts that he wanted. And so that was questionable."

"All these factors added up. Something wasn't right there," says Marsha. "The blood was being mishandled, the evidence was being mishandled, they put into my mind that there is a possibility of cross-contamination. The experts came and explained that, yes, there is contamination here. What I'm saying is that I had doubt that these things could have happened."

Did you know that Mazzola had the same type of blood, the same aliels, that O.J. had? What about the people who were close to the scene who might have had the same type, too? These are the things that I'm tied down with as opposed to the people who just say, well, what about the blood in the Bronco? Like anything else, a discredited witness could have easily done a lot of things.

Let me express the rest of that thought, the idea of tampering

Week of June 26th • Geneticist Bruce Weir is questioned about DNA evidence by defense attorney Peter Neufeld. • Prosecution presents final evidence intended to link O.J. Simpson to the two

with evidence. In my mind, there would not have been a problem for them to have to wait for a blood vial because the crime scene was very bloody. So, if you're going to do something in terms of gathering samples, you could have gotten it from the crime scene. That's no problem. As far as the sock, I'm confused by the sock due to the fact that first there was no blood. First the socks weren't there, then they were there. Then, they came in and showed how this could have been done. How could the blood have gotten on the socks? So much of it? And then you're going to say, "Well, maybe when they did the sample, the phenol test, it was so wet the blood soaked through." Well, really, if you're a good chemist, you shouldn't have had that happen.

Day after day we heard about mixtures of blood. We reviewed the autorads, and there were no problems in any of that information, we understood it thoroughly. Still, I thought that a lot of it was contaminated. I thought also a lot of it was degraded as far as the DNA testing was concerned. I also thought, personally, that blood was planted on the fence simply because when they first made the collections it wasn't there. And I feel that if it was there, whoever did the collecting would have seen it. I cannot understand how, if you are out and you are looking especially for blood drops, you can say, "Oops, I found these on the back of the fence," and then not have somebody look at the whole fence. I would assume that someone would do that. If they didn't, then that tells me somebody did not do a very good job. Then two weeks later you come back and look, and if there is still blood there and you can see it with the naked eye, why wasn't it seen in the beginning? This is not a new fence. This is not a different link of the fence,

murder victims with testimony by L.A.P.D. criminalists Denise Lewis, Susan Brockbank, and Douglas Deedrick, an FBI Special Agent. • **Week of July 3rd** • **The prosecution rests after nearly six months of**

it's on the same property. So personally I felt that the blood was planted.

I had problems understanding how they found the blood smears on the console of the Bronco. Why were they seen after they had torn the inside of this car completely up? They should have been detected immediately. And all of a sudden, you know, a week or so later you are just detecting that. I felt it looked planted. And I also felt that the blood on the glove that was found at Rockingham, I have a problem with understanding why there was so much blood on that glove versus the other glove. There was testimony given on drying time being like three to four hours, and this glove was not collected until seven and a half hours later, I think it was, and it was loaded. It was really bloody.

"Considering where the blood was found and the testimony on the DNA and the aliels and everything, I had no doubt that it was Mr. Simpson's blood," remarks Marsha. "There was no doubt. Now, with it being mishandled, I started having my suspicions on the mishandling of the evidence. But I didn't have any doubts about it being his blood. I have never had any doubt about it being his blood or his type of blood. All the labs that tested the evidence all came up with the same type of aliels, and type of DNA, they all concurred that it was Simpson's blood and Goldman's blood and Nicole's blood all mixed up. I never had any problem with that.

"When I really started having a problem was when the news came about the blood on the glove still being damp. That and the blood on the back fence having more EDTA in it than the blood drops at Bundy. When Mr. Peratis's testimony came up and he

testimony. • **Week of July 10th** • Simpson is described as "pensive and lost in thought" by the pilot of his flight from L.A. to Chicago on the night of the murders. His behavior was friendly, claim two

had testified before the grand jury and, I guess, the preliminary hearings, that he had 7.9 or 8 cc's of blood, but then he comes up with maybe it was more like 6.5, then I started to think, *Well* . . .

"That was one of my turnaround points because there was always talk around about how there was blood missing, there was blood missing, there was blood missing," Marsha continues. "Then you're getting this first blood, what, a week later, two weeks later on the back fence? There was blood on the glove. Then you get the testimony from Peratis that he did collect the 10 cc's, then you get a later video talking about no, well, maybe, I didn't collect 10 cc's. So there is the missing blood. It just started getting sloppy. The criminalists did a bad job. I didn't understand why, when all the bodies and evidence were over at Bundy, why did the criminalist first come to Rockingham where there were just a few drops of blood, while over at Bundy you got all this evidence? To me, the police, the criminalist, they were all just sloppy. It was just a sloppy job."

"I was thinking about the cut on his hand," says Carrie. "Had the cut been as bad as they say it should have been, some of his blood should have been on the Rockingham glove somewhere, but none of his blood was on it. Also, when it came down to whether or not there was some tampering, well, I really feel most of everything after Fuhrman had become a lie. You know, a lot of it I had been questioning. I would say if his finger was cut and he was handling these things—if he was wearing them—his blood should be on one of those gloves. And his blood wasn't on either one of those gloves. The only thing they said that they found on this

autograph seekers, and he did not have visible cuts on his hand. • In a major setback for the defense, Judge Ito rules that they cannot suggest the murders were drug-related. • A doctor claims that

glove was one of his hairs. Now this hair is so small, I mean, one of the hairs off your arm, maybe. I didn't think that was a good effort at collecting the evidence."

I also truly believe that it was Mr. Simpson's blood. Whether it was degraded or not degraded or whatever the situation may be, contaminated or not contaminated, I believe based on the testimony that was given to me that it was Mr. Simpson's blood. However, doubt came in when these other things started happening. The late collection of the blood on the fence. They said everybody's blood may have EDTA in it. How come they didn't find EDTA in Mr. Simpson's blood that they had collected for other samples? So this brought doubt in my mind—that's where a reasonable doubt came in. And then there was all that confusion about how much blood Peratis took. Yes, as far as I'm concerned, Mr. Simpson would have been behind bars if the police work had been done well. But with these other little things that popped up, it caused a doubt.

"In evaluating the evidence that is presented to you in this case, I want to instruct you that you must not be influenced by mere sentiment, conjecture, sympathy, passion, or prejudice . . ."
—Judge Ito's instructions to the jurors on June 9 prior to continuing
grisly testimony over how the murders were committed

The autopsy photos were terrible. That was enough to send everybody out to lunch. Afterward, we had nightmares about them. I couldn't sleep.

Simpson's movements are restricted due to his old football injuries. The doctor also claims that wounds on his hands appear to be from broken glass, not a knife. • **Week of July 17th** • Jury watches an

"I was doing okay with the crime scene photos. But the autopsy photos were bad," remembers Marsha. "And they showed them just before lunch."

"When we went through the autopsy, it was clear that they missed so many points, even though a lot of them were irrelevant," says Carrie. "The people were still dead regardless of how they were killed. And what they were trying to get out of that—the contents of one of the stomachs—could have had some bearing on the case. It was just another mess-up job from leaving the bodies too long."

When asked why the gloves failed to fit O.J. Simpson during the June 15 demonstration staged by the prosecution, Johnnie Cochran says, "I don't think he could act the size of his hands. He would be a great actor if he could act his hands larger."

The glove. Since we've gotten out, we've heard so much about the gloves.

Now, when I saw that demonstration, I thought, *Why in the hell didn't the prosecution try that glove on somebody else that had the same size hands as O.J. before they allowed him to get out here and do this?* I was sick when I saw they didn't fit because I just thought for sure that they were going to fit. I realized that there may have been problems because the glove had been cut up on the inside or because he had on the latex. Common sense could tell you that. The glove was really sort of short.

exercise video in which Simpson jokingly describes accidentally punching "the wife." • **Week of July 24th** • A defense expert describes the presence of a perservative used at the police lab in two samples

"Those gloves fit. He wasn't putting them on right," comments Carrie. "Those were rich leather gloves. That's a piece of leather that stretches. You can do anything with a piece of leather."

Marsha agrees. "Sure, you know, they fit. They were, I shouldn't even say expensive, I should say a good leather glove. And a good leather glove isn't gonna stretch that much. Like a leather shoe. It dries and then it's tight. You put it on and it stretches. He was putting the glove on like this," she says, splaying her fingers. "And I must have had an expression on my face because as he stood there, it was like he was talking to me and he went, 'They don't fit.' They would have fit anybody."

"And the lining was cut up," adds Carrie. "I do believe the gloves fit. I have no doubt about that. The glove demo didn't impress me at all. No, that didn't impress me at all. It didn't work for me. Not one iota. Not one bit."

On June 20, the prosecution team shifts its strategy and drops plans to present additional testimony on domestic violence.

One of the most confusing aspects of the trial in hindsight was why the prosecution didn't introduce additional evidence about O.J. abusing Nicole.

I did consider the evidence of the episode where O.J. abused his wife and then pleaded no contest. But basically I considered it because I knew that the prosecution was trying to make that a

of blood recovered from the crime scene. The presence of this preservative proves that the blood was planted by police, claims the defense. • A forensics expert for the defense claims the blood on

motive in this particular case. But I could not consider it as a heavy motive in terms of him building up some type of rage because of the time period we heard testimony about. If it had been something a little more consistent—because we went from '85 to '89 and then from '89 to '93—I would have looked at it differently. But based on what we saw in the evidence, I could not lay a heavy consideration as far as that being a motive. I feel that if a person is capable of extreme rage, then these types of things happen a bit more often than maybe once every four or five years.

"I'm not going to sit here and tell you that I didn't give it much weight. But I will tell you that they presented to me, what, one case?" asks Marsha. "There was the case when Fuhrman came and O.J. had beat up the car. Then there was the case when she ran out of the house, and then there was Denise saying they were sitting around and he pushed them all out of the house. And then there was the time he grabbed her crotch. Now, if you put all of those together, they were always drunk. Both of them, all of them. They were always drinking. Here they are, drinking, tempers are flaring, and I think Nicole was a little scrapper herself, not so quick to sit down.

"My husband is 6'1" and weighs 210. I had jumped on him one evening. He did something I didn't like—I didn't want him to drive my car or something. I snatched my keys from him. And he said, 'Oh, girl, go on now. Go on.' I think that you can have too many drinks and tempers can flare and things happen. See, that's what I related that to. Alcohol-induced rages. Still, that's no excuse. But I do believe that alcohol had a lot to do with the four incidents they presented to me. Now that's all I know about. And

the sock found in Simpson's house was not splattered but applied through direct compression.
• **Week of July 31st** • Defense expert John Gerdes testifies that chronic contamination problems

so, when they went from '89 to '92 or '93 when he came through the door—you know, the 911 tape—there was no abuse there. He hadn't hit her or anything, but he did scare her. He would scare me, too. But there was no abuse there. What they presented to me, well, I related it all to they had been drinking. They were drunk. One of them said something to the other one that he or she didn't like. So, actually, her being as thin as she is, if he gripped her like this, it would leave a bruise. But I didn't think it was necessarily a motive for murder."

I have never in my life seen that type of attitude from anybody. I've heard of people who accept that. They think, *I've done something wrong so I guess he has the right to hit me.* That type of stuff infuriates me. Nobody has the right to put his or her hands on anybody as far as I'm concerned. I can't relate to it and it makes me angry to think there are people out there who can relate to it. But if that's their choice, that's their choice.

"Well, it was stated that maybe black women do not look at spousal abuse as seriously as white women," says Carrie. "But I say women are women and abuse is abuse. I divorced my husband after three years because he came home and jumped on me and I left. I never went back. But there are women who believe that their men hit them but really don't mean it. Whether it's black or white, Asian, Hispanic, it doesn't matter—they believe, 'He loves me. He's not going to do it again. He didn't really mean it.' I really believe it all depends on the female herself. I don't think race has anything to do with it. I believe it's the woman herself. It's just like some men have the same problem. They have women who

plague the L.A.P.D. crime lab. • **Week of August 7th** • A pathologist testifies for the defense that the victims struggled violently for their lives and could have been attacked by more than one assailant. •

fight them. I really believe from my heart that that's the way it is. I would not stay and be whipped.

"I can only speak on the part they gave us," Carrie continues. "The part they gave us was it had occurred but it ceased to exist as far as physical abuse. But verbal abuse was still there in '93. Verbal abuse can take a person down, but you had an opportunity to ignore verbal abuse by doing what she did, call 911. And if she was being abused, there were certain things she should have done as far as I'm concerned. If I were Nicole I would have taken a piece out of him. If you want to pick up the kids, we'll meet someplace neutral. But that's me."

After presenting 58 witnesses and 488 exhibits, the state rests its case on July 6.

It sort of went back and forth the whole way through. Sometimes I felt that the prosecution's presentation of the evidence and exhibits was so strong that, yeah, maybe he did do it. Then, at one point, I thought, *Well, if he didn't do it, he knows who did do it.* That was more or less my final thing. If he did not do it, maybe he knows who did. But I was not there to do my own personal judgment and I really had to stay focused on the evidence. I constantly kept telling myself, "Stay focused. Keep your mind on the real deal here, what's happening here." If you allowed yourself to drift off for a minute, pretty soon you're not hearing anything but what you want to hear, bringing into the database things that you

Week of August 14th • The prosecution fears that Judge Ito cannot remain impartial in the trial due to remarks made by Furhman about his wife. • Judge John Reid, who is called in to rule on the Fuhrman

want to hear. If you feel in your mind that he is guilty, whatever testimony comes up, you're just going to pick up the guilty portion and that's all you're going to do. I tried extremely hard to keep all the evidence in mind and tried to weigh it appropriately.

It's a very tragic case and I still feel sorry for the people who lost loved ones. I truly do. I just did what I had to do. I just worked with what they gave me. And I never put any more thought to it than that. It was a murder case. There was a man on trial. I didn't put any name to it, no notoriety. The man was accused of murdering two people.

"All through the trial you had ups and downs," Carrie agrees. "They said there's a blood trail and that he had plenty of time to do this. Then when the police get on the witness stand, they contradict themselves. During the time the blood was found at Bundy it was looking strong against O.J. The FBI was talking about the Bruno Magli shoes and the hair and all of these things. This was looking terrible for O.J. But then this is when another change came. They turn around and bring in a guy from New York or Chicago where O.J. was supposed to have purchased some shoes. They didn't really go anywhere with that shoe deal. That guy had the shoe prints, but they couldn't do anything with them. It was like that all the way. You never knew what was coming next and so you couldn't just make up your mind."

"My doubt was over the time. I didn't think one man could have done all that damage in that length of time and get back to the house without help," says Marsha. "And they kept saying that he did it alone. That he did all this all by himself. I kept saying, 'I just don't see how that could happen.' Maybe that was my biggest

tapes, does not foresee Judge Ito's wife being called as a witness and rules that Ito should remain as the judge in the case. • **Week of August 21st** • Dr. Henry Lee testifies that imprints on Goldman's

thing. The time frame bothered me. I just had too many questions. Driving up there with the shovel. So what did he do? Take the shovel and go to the back of the house and dig a hole and bury the clothes? He didn't have that much time by himself and they never presented to me that he had any help. Then, on the other hand, what happened to those dark clothes he was wearing at the recital? I was really stuck for a while."

I have not declared him innocent at all. I truly believe he knows something about it. Whenever I sat in the courtroom I made a conscious effort not to make eye contact with O.J. The only ones I made eye contact with were the attorneys and the media. I started doing that in the latter part of the trial. At first I tried to keep my head down but I started getting knots in the back of my neck. One day I just happened to catch O.J.'s eye. I truly, truly, truly just wanted to ask, "Did you do this? Did you absolutely do this?" I looked at him and I would just turn my head. He would get like a little slight smile. Just slight.

"What I would say was that he was out of it," Arnelle Simpson says on July 10 when asked about her father's reaction to hearing about the murders. "He was shocked, dazed."

I had no problem with Arnelle. She just basically reported how the officers approached her and how she received the information that Nicole was dead. And then she tried to locate her father. She just reported things as she saw them or as she was directed. Same

jeans could be from a print different than that of the Italian shoe that left the bloody footprints, helping to advance the theory that there may have been two killers. • In further testimony, Lee says that there is

with Shirley Baker—O.J.'s sister—and his mother. They just reported what they knew.

Once the defense came on, we heard from a whole list of people pretty quickly. Some of them testified as character witnesses, others testified about the timeline of the murders that the prosecution had developed.

"Like that guy from the American Psychological Association who played golf with O.J.—McKay?" remembers Marsha. "Well, he just reported what he saw, too, the fact that they played golf. Waste of time. And the fact that O.J. was happy-go-lucky, but he would have been because he was there to represent Hertz. So naturally he would be happy-go-lucky."

Then there was Mandel, the guy who walked with his date on his way home near Nicole's at about ten twenty-five. They had said that they did not see any blood, but I didn't think that they would have seen any blood because they were too busy trying to communicate with each other. I don't know at that particular time if the blood trail had flowed out that far. But I did think that maybe they should have seen some dog prints or something. And I was trying to remember back when I was young and dating and what I did on a date. I sort of pictured them maybe looking down and just walking. I felt that they were being honest and believable.

"And don't forget the Tillander lady," Carrie points out. "She was the one who set up a time record. The time the lady left her house and all that. She was reporting what she thought."

Then there was Robert Heidstra, the one who walks his dogs at night. He had the two old dogs. I sort of felt he was believable,

"something wrong" with the handling of blood samples collected at the murder site. • **Week of August 28th** • The Mark Fuhrman tapes are played in open court (jury not present). In an emotional

but what happened is he got caught up in a situation where he started running off at the mouth, and somewhere along the line someone told him he can make all this money, and he started saying that this is what he is going to do. I figured this man walked his dog every night at the same time. He seems like the type who would be consistent in what he says and what he does. He was the one who heard the voice, "Hey, hey, hey." He never said it was a white Bronco. He said it could have been. At first, he said a Cherokee or something and he said he saw it going the opposite way. I sort of believed him. I don't know what it was that made me believe him but I did. And all the people at the airport— the baggage employee, the airplane captain, the other passenger who asked for an autograph—they were all believable.

O.J.'s physician, Dr. Huizenga, was also very impressive, very knowledgeable, a very successful doctor. I believed him as far as his examination, but the hairdresser, Juanita Moore . . . ?

"Waste of time, to me," Carrie assesses. "I guess they were trying to find out something about some dandruff or something. Some of that stuff was truly a waste of time. They got away from the key issues with some of these people. Like the musical lady. No problem with her, but my first impression was, well, why is she here? Just to say that he was at this party and he was in this great mood? That really didn't mean anything to me. What did that have to do with the homicide? Same with the interior designer. I could care less if he's getting his house redesigned. I guess it was to prove that he and Paula had a relationship at a certain period of time. But that was not even necessary. You knew

press conference, Fred Goldman says, "There was no reason to have two hours of this hate spewed out over the public airways. My son, Nicole, and her family have a right to a fair trial and this is not fair."

they had a relationship. They had one off and on even, I guess, during the time he and Nicole were married. So that was a waste of time."

After all these people came through, I was surprised that we never heard from Faye Resnick. Eventually, I came to the conclusion that Faye Resnick wasn't going to be used because they said she was in drug rehabilitation. I'm not talking about some junkie who doesn't have two cents, who would run over you with a truck and steal your money to get a fix. This is somebody who did have money and lived in Beverly Hills and did a little cocaine, as so many people in Hollywood do. But I guess they didn't want to bring all that drug activity into the trial.

> *"He might have had the body of Tarzan, but he walked like Tarzan's grandfather."*
>
> —Dr. Wayne Huizenga testifying on July 14
> about O.J. Simpson's arthritis

I also have arthritis, and I can tell you that it is a painful condition. I do take medication for it. I think that if O.J. had been in pain then, he definitely could not have killed them. But, arthritis notwithstanding, if you're not in pain, then it's not going to stop you from killing anybody. The pain comes and goes. What got me is that basically they were talking about arthritis in the man's legs. The knees. It's not his knees and legs that hold the knife.

"I'm not saying that he could not have held the knife," adds

• **Week of September 4th** • Excerpts from Mark Fuhrman's tapes are played for the jury. Two women testify that they heard Fuhrman use racial epithets in the past. • Fuhrman invokes the Fifth

Carrie. "I'm saying that if you have arthritis in your joints, and you're out there forty-odd years old and you're wrestling with a young man twenty-some years old who is supposed to be very active, I think you're going to have some bruises. But I was confused over what O.J. said during that exercise video. I would love for them to play that tape back. I could swear I heard O.J. say, 'You better be glad your wife is not doing this exercise.'

That's what I thought, too. With all those advertisements—the video and the Juice Plus ads—I was thinking that if this product did all of this and worked the way he said it does, then he shouldn't have any arthritic pain now. He shouldn't be having any physical ailments since he has this stuff that is supposed to be dynamite. I think a lot of those entertainers and actors are liars. It's all about dollars and cents."

"Shit, I'd be sitting up there saying how great this stuff is, too, if they paid me," admits Marsha.

"The exact words I don't know, but it was something to the effect that he went over there as Mr. Simpson was the suspect."

—Larry Fiato, organized crime informant in the federal witness protection program, testifying on September 19 on comments made to him by Detective Vannatter

When the Fiato brothers walked into the courtoom, I was on the edge of my seat. After I found out that they were informants, I

Amendment when asked if he gave truthful testimony, had ever falsified a police report, or planted evidence in the Simpson case. Jury is not present. •

figured, well, at any given time anybody can come out here and try to knock these guys off. I got the feeling it was some sort of Italian Mafia group. When these people want to knock somebody off, outside of being in heaven and hell, you can't hide. I was too busy looking at the door and checking things out to really listen to what the hell they were even talking about on the stand.

I figured they didn't have much to say anyway, other than the fact that they heard Vannatter say O.J. was a suspect. All the rest of that stuff was immaterial to me. I was checking out all three doors of the courtroom at all times and I'm sitting on the edge of my seat. Honest. Because I know this is the United States of America and I know people come up missing and you figure these informants have been in the witness protection program for, what, twelve years? But that's got to be up soon and I figured it could happen right here, so I have to be ready. Prepared to run, jump.

I really didn't believe their testimony, I did believe they were all sitting there drinking and talking about whatever case they're involved in now and information came up about the O.J. case. I don't care where you are or who you're talking to, this O.J. Simpson case just always seems to come up in a conversation. I believe they were sitting there and talking about it, but I thought that he was lying. I also thought that, as an experienced detective, Vannatter should have kept things more confidential.

"If it doesn't fit, you must acquit."

—Johnnie Cochran to the jury on September 25
as part of his closing argument

Week of September 11th • A former executive of Aris Isotoner testifies that he is "100 percent certain" that Simpson wore the same kind of gloves that were found on the murder scene. He noted that

Although we all thought Marcia Clark did an excellent job, a few of us had problems with her attitude. I think she presented her case well. It was a little drawn out and, at that point, all I really wanted was for them to do what they came there to do: Give the closing argument, review what we had gone over, present whatever evidence they wanted to present, and just be done with it. But that last little tear-jerker thing she had going there, I didn't care for. I felt for the Goldmans and the Browns. That was tough. One of the toughest days I had. It was like the autopsy photos. I couldn't believe somebody could have done that to those people. Damn! They almost cut off those folks' heads. How could somebody just stand there and just absolutely cut somebody's head off? It was heart-wrenching.

Near the end of Marcia Clark's closing argument, one of the jurors broke down and cried. It was such an emotional speech. I thought, *Jesus Christ. Please. Somebody help me. Get these people to understand that I am not totally illiterate here. That we don't need this.* And I know it's part of the game, but we didn't need this emotional appeal in order for us to reach a decision.

The only thing I didn't like about Marcia was her expressions. She had a strong case. She believed in her case. Maybe she was just showing me that she was frustrated. I know it was a long, long trial and I know she worked late, I assume, because she looked very tired sometimes. Sometimes, she looked terrible. She would just get too frustrated. She's got to stop doing that emotion thing. Just believe in what she's doing. And I'm sure she does. Just believe in what she's doing and she'd do just fine.

That would be my only criticism of her. And that was based on

this type of glove was "quite rare." • An FBI expert testifies that a blood print on Goldman's jeans appears to have been made by his shirt and not by the shoe of a second attacker, as proposed by the

how she projected her examinations with the witnesses. It made it seem like we were on a different level. I know everybody doesn't have a college degree, but there's such a thing as common sense. If I've said it once, I've said it ten times: Don't leave your common sense outside the door. Bring in your gut feeling. Somehow I think Marcia felt we hadn't, and I think that was her downfall. If she would have trusted us and kept her common sense, I think maybe it would have gone a different way. That's based on a lot of things I've heard and things I've later learned the prosecution chose to leave out because they thought that we could not deal with it, or we would not understand it, or the defense team would turn it around a different way.

After we got out, I was surprised to learn that everybody thought we bought all of that showboating from Johnnie Cochran. Let's set the record straight. Maybe if I'd been sequestered for two weeks, that stuff would have been okay. But after nine months, honey, I don't need that. All I need from you is a complete outline of all the evidence of what the defense had to offer, what the prosecution had to offer, and let me regroup my notes in my mind and see if I'm on the right track here. Because that stuff sort of throws you off. I don't need that part of the drama. And nobody else did and I made sure because we talked about it in deliberations. "Girl, do you believe that shit? Did you see that hat routine? I nearly died. What the hell was that?" You know, that type of thing.

"The only thing Mr. Cochran did for me in his closing argument was help me recollect a lot of things," Marsha relates. "When I went back into the deliberation room there were things I wanted to pinpoint and go over in my notes. That was the only

defense. • **Week of September 18th** • The prosecution calls its last rebuttal witness. • Larry and Craig Fiato testify about conversations with Detective Vannatter. • The jury hears testimony

thing his closing argument did for me. He didn't impress me at all. It was just too flamboyant for me."

When Johnnie Cochran put that hat on his head, everybody wanted to die. You could see stomachs literally moving. He's looking like a damn fool standing up there. Stomachs are moving, trying to contain the laughter. We're laughing because he thinks he's got you. He knew he was on TV. He did not have me on his side. I cannot speak for the other jurors, but the only thing he could have done for me was sit his ass down. He was performing. I don't have anything against the man. He was doing his job. But I wasn't there for a performance. Just show me what you've got and let me take it from there. There's no need for you to get out here for me and do seal acts. You don't need to be tooting horns and blowing whistles. Just show me what you've got here and I'll do my job."

The whole thing with those closing arguments was I felt it was all a script. Everybody had his or her little script. I hated it because at that point you're supposed to be tying in all the evidence and tying in everything. So you're sitting there and trying to just focus on the issues and here they are, Marcia Clark, the woe-is-me and blah, blah, blah, trying to get the tear thing. And Johnnie Cochran is going on about Proverbs and this, that, and the other, and the hat routine, and "If it doesn't fit, you must acquit." You don't need all of that. We tried to wash all of that out and just hear what we needed to hear. We hated it. When we brought up the subject everybody said, "God, was that the most miserable thing you ever had to deal with in your life?"

Johnnie Cochran is an excellent communicator. He has that

from the final witness. • **Week of September 25th** • Closing arguments commence. Marcia Clark begins, and is followed by Christopher Darden. • Johnnie Cochran and Barry Scheck

ability. But in this case, I was more supportive of Marcia Clark. I thought that she came across as a much stronger, much more together attorney. Maybe I'm being a bit prejudiced because she was a woman. I don't know. This is my honest opinion. I don't think he was a better storyteller because those kinds of stories don't affect me. I was there to review the evidence. That's all I cared about. I thought the prosecution had outstanding evidence, but there was a breakdown in the way it was gathered and preserved. It wasn't the prosecution's fault. They did a hell of a job with what they had.

I mean that. I truly think that they did a good job. I believe their support was poor, where they received their information from. There was a breakdown. That was it. They did the best they could. And now that we're out, all I'm hearing is, "Let's all put the blame where it belongs, saying the jury this, the jury that. The jury didn't understand the DNA process. The jury didn't understand." The jury understood a hell of a lot more than people think they understood. People think that because we didn't stay locked up in that room as long as they thought we should, we must have had a lack of understanding or we rushed to judgment. The judgment was not rushed. There was more than enough time to put into our judgment. These same people who are jumping on us need to jump on some legislation to change some of this judicial law they have out there. That's where the fight has to begin. Not with us. We can't take the burden. We're taking the burden from the NOW (National Organization for Women) organization. When I signed up for jury duty, I didn't see the State of California versus NOW, the State of California versus Racism, the State of California

put on the defense's closing arguments. •
Marcia Clark and Christopher Darden give their
rebuttal to the defense's closing arguments. •
Monday, October 2nd • Jury deliberates for

versus all these things. All I saw was the State of California versus Orenthal James Simpson. Out of this, we got political wars. We got wars with battered women's organizations. We got wars with the judicial system. We're hearing that we set this world back on its toes from square one. The hell if we have. These things have always been here. They have always been here camouflaged. Don't blame us.

four hours and reaches a verdict. • **Tuesday, October 3rd** • ''Not guilty'' verdict is announced and Simpson goes free.

8

THE ELECTION

—————

Once closing arguments had come to an end on Friday and we received Judge Ito's instructions, we entered the deliberation room. It's really the jury room, but it's also called the deliberation room. It's behind the courtroom on the ninth floor. Upon entering, we all sat at our seats that we normally sit in every day. See, during the time we were there, we would each sit in the same spot basically all the time.

After we sat down around the table, a few questions came up as to how we were going to go about picking a foreman. Nothing complicated, just basic things like, well, were we going to draw straws, or were we going to make nominations and vote by ballot or a show of hands? I was caught off guard when Carrie jumped up and said she wanted to nominate #230, which is my number.

"When the judge first told us we could retire and go in and select our foreman, I went into the room and I spoke right up," says Carrie. "I came right out and said, 'Okay, we have to nominate someone for foreman. I nominate Armanda Cooley, #230.' Then two or three other people nodded in agreement and said, 'Oh, yes,' and then someone seconded the nomination. But rather than calling it a done deal, I asked if anyone else wanted to nominate someone. Then #1290, Anise, said, 'Yes. I would like to nominate Lon, #247.' So now there were two nominations and I asked everyone if there was anyone else they would like to see as foreman. No one else said anything. Then I said, 'Well, we'll have to take a vote on this. All for Armanda, hold up their hands.' So we did it by a show of hands."

"We were sitting around the big table when all the people who wanted to vote for Armanda raised their hands," Marsha explains. "I believe the vote was 6–3 because I don't recall seeing #19, David Aldana, raising his hand and voting at all. Armanda and Lon didn't vote. Then we asked, 'All for Lon.' When that vote was counted, there were four people for Lon. This is the way it went. After the votes everyone sat around the table and said, 'Well, we've got Armanda.' Lon congratulated Armanda. We all laughed. We chatted. We knew what we wanted.

"By now we've all heard about how everyone has criticized us for being so fast, saying that we're the speedy jurors and all," says Carrie. "But as far as I'm concerned, let's just say we were there nine months and we knew what we had to do. I've been in a back room before. I knew who I wanted to nominate. So I nominated Armanda, and fortunately someone else was nominated, too. We took our vote and that was the end of that. There wasn't any need to go over anyone's life history and what they had devoted to the trial."

I think the reason why they picked me was because I am the type of person who always takes the negative aspect of an issue and tries to turn it into something positive. I'm the one knocking on the door to get them up to go to church on Sunday. I'm the one saying, "Look, it's going to be all right. We don't have long to go. We have less time than we had when we came in here January 11." You know, just the type of person who tries to give that positive get-up-and-go to people who are having a hard time. I guess you could say that the mothering instinct in my personality is quite strong and that's just how a lot of people saw me. They still respected me for who I was, because in life you'll always need somebody who's going to see something through with a positive attitude. I really think this is the reason why I was chosen to be the foreman.

"As for myself, I chose Armanda due to the fact that she was even-keeled. She conversed with all of us. She was able to talk to all of us. I thought she was quite intelligent," Carrie adds. "Not that all of them weren't, but I thought she was more able to keep a quiet room. I am glad I wasn't the foreperson because I have a tendency to speak out. I'm the first to admit there are times when maybe I shouldn't speak, that there are times when I should be listening. She just seemed to be the ideal person. Her attitude was such a nice one. She just had a nice charisma about her. And I think everyone else could see that, too."

Right after the vote was taken, Carrie reached over and hit the buzzer to call the deputy. She was the closest one to it. I think someone made a statement along the lines of "Okay, now we're shaking and moving," or something like that. I don't think there were any frowns or comments. As a matter of fact, Lon came up and hugged and congratulated me. I told him at the time, "I need all the help I can get." He said, "No problem. No problem." And here's a guy who hardly ever spoke to anybody. I mean he would speak as part of the general conversation, but he never really got involved with anybody. I was surprised and touched that he made that statement to me because he sort of alienated himself. He never wanted to get involved in anything. If you wanted to ask the judge about anything, you couldn't include him. He just wanted to keep his space. I guess maybe that's why a lot of people were surprised when Ann nominated Lon. I think a lot of folks were sitting there thinking, *Where did that come from?* But I understood why. It was because he had previous experience as the foreman on the last case he was on and that would have qualified him for the job.

So Carrie buzzed and Deputy Dinwiddie came in and just said, "Already? You did it, huh?" And we told him what the decision was and said, "We're ready." And that was it. We waited around because we thought we were going to go back to court. The wait was quite a bit, I would say probably fifteen to twenty minutes. But we didn't go back into the court. The deputy came back and said, "You're going home." And that was it. We were taken back to the hotel.

I took my role as foreman quite seriously. I felt it was important to be a leader and to be fair and make sure that everyone had the same information with which to make a decsion. If there's testimony that I heard and there was confusion about it, I felt it was my job to wash out all the garbage and keep everyone focused on the basic information. It's my job to spread that information to the other eleven jurors once we get in that deliberation room. It's my job to say, "Well, Mike, you really didn't hear what she was saying. What she is saying was that O.J. made a drug deal. He paid $100 for this crystal. This stuff has a tendency of making you mad, changing your whole disposition, putting you into a rage. You didn't really hear what she was saying because you were angry." That type of thing. Make people see. That's the whole idea of deliberating, helping people understand what they didn't pick up. You've got to wash out all that garbage. And once I felt we had a clear picture of what went on, that's when I decided to take a vote.

9

A RUSH TO JUDGMENT?

―――

Ladies and gentlemen, as you've—I've indicated to you, you are not to discuss this case while you are away from the jury room. Your jury deliberations may only take place while all twelve of you are assembled in the jury room. In other words, when you go back to the hotel when we conclude for the day and during the course of any recess, you may not discuss amongst yourselves the facts and circumstances of the case. You may not conduct any deliberations when you're at the hotel or anywhere in between.
—JUDGE LANCE ITO

October 2, 1995

Faced with the upcoming deliberation as foreman, I was more preoccupied with the case than usual. But when I went back to my hotel room and lay in the bed and tried to rest, I found I couldn't sleep. All I could do was just go over and over in my head what had occurred, who said what, what happened here, what happened there. There were even times I sat and broke down the time period of what people had to say, even though we didn't have our notebooks in our room. But whenever we had free time through-out the course of the trial, like when everybody would be at the sidebar, I'd flip through the pages of my notes to review what was said. Or if something had come to my mind during the night as I lay awake quietly deliberating, I would go back the next day and check the notes I had taken.

Over the weekend, everyone had begun to pack their things up. I know there were a lot of reports about how we had packed up before we even went into deliberation, as if it were a sign that our minds were already made up, but it wasn't because we were ready to leave. Once closing arguments started, the sheriffs had told us that we should begin to send things home with our fami-lies and visitors when they came on Saturday or Sunday. But after I was elected on Friday and deliberations were to begin on Mon-day, they stopped the Saturday conjugal visit. Our families were allowed to visit on Sunday as usual, but they were all put together in a single room. Some of the jurors had made arrangements for their spouses or significant others or family members to pick up most of their luggage, because we had to get as much of that stuff out of the hotel as we possibly could. Remember, we had been there a long time and most of us had made every effort to make our rooms as much like home as possible. So everyone got all of their suits, dress items, and court items and set them aside to go home. Basically, what we kept was just jeans and T-shirts and things like that. Everything else was slated to go home. That's the reason why everyone was packing.

Personally, I figured that deliberations would go on for a cou-ple of weeks. And that was because of other trials I had heard about. But then I thought about some of those trials. A lot of them prolonged the time because they supposedly wanted to take an extra day or two away from the job. Well, we sure didn't have to deal with that type of issue. Another thing is that in many cases you've only been together as a jury for a few days, a few weeks, maybe a month, and you're often deliberating and communicating with people you don't even know. After all that time, we had come to know each other the way family members do. Still, I thought that it was going to take some time.

On Saturday, I took advantage of the opportunity to go with Marsha up to Buttonwillow, California, where her son lives. It was her grandson's first birthday, and she had sworn that she wasn't going to miss it for the world. She had arranged to go some months ago, not having any idea that it would be the weekend before deliberations were to begin, and she had asked me to come. I think that if Judge Ito had known the timing in advance, he would have said no, but he had given his word and so we went. Considering the pressure, it was a nice break.

"That Saturday, September 29, I went to visit my son, Kevin, up in Buttonwillow," Marsha explains. "It was my grandson Kevin Jr.'s first birthday and most of my family was going to be there. Even though I had no idea that we were still going to be involved in the trial, I had asked permission from Judge Ito some months before if I could go and he said yes. Since this boy had been growing up without his grandma, I sure wasn't going to let them stop me from going.

"I had asked Armanda to come, too. We left early Saturday morning with two deputies who drove us up to Buttonwillow in a van. I tried to put all of the thoughts of the trial behind me and just focused on enjoying my grandson that day. I didn't want to think about the fact that come Monday morning someone's life was going to be in my hands. I tried to forget as much as I could, even though I had two deputies there. All I wanted to do was enjoy the day and my family and my little grandson. Since he had been born just a few months before I was sequestered, he didn't recognize me, but it was wonderful all the same.

"I wasn't preoccupied with the case that weekend, but being with my family helped. They never mentioned a single word during the day and neither did I. Everybody knew what was going on, but it was just so good to see them and that little boy that the trial never came up. I did not think about Mr. Simpson in particular, but I did wonder how he felt about his life being in the hands of twelve people. But my mind was clear. All I wanted to do was get in there Monday morning and start deliberating over the evidence."

"I really can't tell you how O.J. might have been feeling that weekend, but had I been O.J. I probably would have been very, very nervous," says Carrie. "I say that because I don't think he could ever guess how we were thinking or how we felt about what we were hearing. As far as I'm concerned, I never gave him an inkling of what I thought or looked at him as if I sympathized with him. It was just that simple: I had to do what I had to do. Had I found him guilty, as opposed to finding him not guilty, that is what I would have had to do. I came to do what I had to do regardless of whom it may have hurt or helped.

"I also thought about both the Browns and the Goldmans. Were they nervous? Afraid? Terrified? I don't know, but I certainly don't think they were happy. I believe they were probably quite depressed. Most of us were depressed because this was not a happy mode. This was a depressed state. The mere thought that I had to be there, making this kind of decision, in this kind of role, was not a happy one. I often asked the Lord to help me because there was a time when I thought about that place in the Bible where it says, 'Judge ye not.' It really came to a point where I was wondering, *Carrie, are you really doing the right thing? Should you be the one here to say whether or not this person did that or this person did not do this?* But I prayed and the Lord answered my prayer because I feel my decision was fair. With the jurors, I felt we were only as strong as our weakest link. This is the way life goes.

"There was so much tension in the air, I literally had headaches, could not eat, could not sleep. I was nervous. The sheriffs had told us to pack it up and that's what people concentrated on. You could hear us all going back and forth in the hall: 'Oh, I've got one suitcase ready. I'm about to get the rest of it.' 'I don't know what I'm going to wear tomorrow.' 'I've got everything packed. I wonder if they want us to leave this?' There were a lot of questions we asked each other as far as the packing and moving around went. It helped occupy our minds.

"The deputies were more serious than ever that weekend, and they let us know. 'We will call your family for you. We will let them know how you feel, but there will not be any conjugal visits on Saturday,' they said. They tried to do the best they could with us because we had been there for months. We sort of understood each other. We knew the deputies were there to do a job and we respected that. They were quite professional people and I think they understood the pressure we were under."

When we walked into the deliberation room on Monday morning, I was a little concerned. I was the foreman and, see, you don't get any instructions at first. Judge Ito went over some basic rules but said he would send in the written instructions later. Let's get the record straight. I had no experience. But, luckily, my first statement was, "We're gathered here united as one. I personally am going to need all the help I can get. I don't have any direct experience in this. Number two, I expect everybody to be civil to each other. We're all adults. I expect you to treat the next person that has the floor in the same manner or demeanor that you want to be treated. So I would appreciate any assistance or help that anyone can give me."

I openly asked for help because one of the jurors had been on jury duty eight times and another one had been four or five times. And I think Brenda had been several times. So I was surprised when the first thing that was raised was the question of taking a vote by secret ballot. At first I was not going to do that because I didn't think we would be allowed to do it. I remembered something in the jury instructions, something about we weren't allowed to do something when taking a vote. I could not exactly put it straight in my head. A couple of other people thought that way as well. So my immediate decision was to take the vote but not count it until I clarify what I'm thinking.

So that's what we did. It turned out there was a section in the instructions about not taking straw votes on decisions to be made, but it didn't say anything about a secret ballot. After we took the secret ballot, it came back ten not guilty, two guilty. I reconfirmed that by having somebody else count it. When we started deliberations, one of the things that I stated was that I am the type of person who stands by her convictions. I don't give a damn if we're going to be in here the next nine months. I am going to fight for what I believe in and for what I'm saying until somebody can prove me otherwise. Therefore, if anybody around this table is going to have a problem with that, then we need to discuss that first because I wanted everybody to stand by what he or she believed in. I felt that was the only way we could reach a fair verdict.

"I was surprised myself because I expected us to be in there bumping against each other, disagreeing and all of this, especially when we got started," admits Carrie. "It was Monday morning and I was surprised about a lot of things. Surprised as the devil that both the prosecuting and the defense side had retired. Surprised that we didn't get a long list of instructions to start with. The judge just said, 'Okay, you can go in the deliberating room. We have papers to give you later. But while you are in the deliberating room, we'll have these papers drawn up.' Mrs. Robertson, who was the clerk of the court, was going to take care of that. So we went into our deliberation room and we looked at each other, knowing that Armanda was the foreman, and wondered what to do next.

"I told her, 'Well, Armanda, all the times I've been coming in here, the first thing we did was to find out how everybody felt. We must find out how we feel so we know where we are going.' Lon said, 'I served as a foreperson before and we always took a silent vote as to how people felt so we knew how we were going.' Then Brenda Moran spoke out: 'Yes, I've worked on a jury before, too. And we did vote.' But Brenda never did come up with the idea. It wasn't her decision to help Armanda. We were all in there putting our part in. That's what it takes in the back room. That's what I call it: the back room. The deliberating room. Everybody. It wasn't one. It wasn't two. It wasn't nine. It was twelve. It took all of us to get where we had to get to make a decision. So, when Brenda finally spoke, we all spoke. There were some who said, 'Oh no, we can't vote. How are we going to vote so no one knows?' We had to tell them that it's not that you're going to write your name on it. It's not that anyone is going to read what you said. It's just private. No one will know who voted what. All we're going to do is just write on a little piece of paper *guilty* or *not guilty*. And place it in a jar or hat and find out what and how each of us felt.

"They got the candy jar. We had eaten so much candy during this deliberation. The office clerks did keep us up with a lot of candy. Armanda says, 'Each of us will take a small piece of paper and write how we feel. Guilty or not guilty.' At that time, my back was against the blackboard anyway and I always loved to play on the blackboard. I would draw little happy faces on the blackboard. 'Have a nice day.' Just things to amuse each of us and so I took it upon myself to stand at the blackboard and Armanda said, 'Carrie, you will write them as I call them off.' Everybody had dropped their vote in this little candy dish. It was ten not guilty, two guilty. We went back over it again. It came up ten-two again.

"After we all had voted again, there was a knock at the door. Mrs. Robertson wheeled in a cart with about ten or eleven of the blue hard-back folders that were filled with pictures we had seen in court. They were small photos of the big evidence charts we had seen. She also brought some papers and these papers consisted of what we wanted to see. There was a form we could use to request what kind of evidence we wanted to hear. They were given to the foreperson, Armanda."

Carrie continues. "Once this material was in, we began to deliberate. First, it was about how we felt. I can't say exactly who came up with the first question, but the ones who said he was guilty did not speak out and say, 'I feel he is guilty because of such and such a thing.' That never did come up. We put all our questions and statements on the table. My whole thing was I wanted to be able to live with myself. There were things I really wanted to talk about. There were things I was sure everyone else wanted to talk about.

"At this time, two or three people said, 'Yes, I want to see the thing about the time.' I think Marsha was one of them. And then there were Lon and Dave. Dave spoke out about the knuckles of Ron Goldman. If Ron didn't come in contact with a person, why would his knuckles be bruised like that? Dave studied karate, and he knew that you can make contact with somebody and bruise your knuckle in that way. Gina went on about the glove. We went to the books. First we took out one or two of them and, after so many questions came up, Armanda said, 'Well, we'll just pass them all out. We gave each one of the jurors a book. Each one was going through evidence. If there was a question that popped up about the time or the wailing dog, footprints, the glove, each one would say, 'Well, I have the book on the glove.' It was like brainstorming. That's exactly the word I've been looking for. We went through each other's brains. We knew what we felt. We knew what we were looking for. Now, we're in here about four hours with you going over things that you've gone over for nine months in your head. Everybody went over evidence each day. As we got it, we went through it. Because you had nothing else to do. You couldn't crochet all night. This is what put you to sleep or kept you up. There was many a night I didn't sleep. This is why we were able to talk about it, put it on the table, and make a decision."

"That's what everyone really wants to know, what went on in the deliberation room," says Marsha. "From my point of view there were twelve educated people in there making a decision. Twelve people whom Marcia Clark and Johnnie Cochran selected. We went in there and we sat down at the table and the foreman stood up and said that she wanted us all to be able to work together in a human manner. This was her first time being a fore-man and it was her first time serving on a jury. She had heard horror stories, just like Carrie, myself, and a whole lot of other people had. But we were all in agreement that we would work together and that each person would have a chance to talk. If one person didn't agree with the other, we would hear each one out. Of course, now we'd been together for nine months so I don't understand why people would think we wouldn't be able to work together.

"Armanda, our foreman, asked if anyone had ever deliberated before. Lon had, Ann, #1290, had, and so had #795, Brenda. Ar-manda had asked for any type of assistance that they could offer and then asked about the order of how it was supposed to go. The clerk, Deirdre Robertson, had come in earlier and brought us all the condensed versions of all the evidence. All those big boards and all the crime scene photos, all the autopsy photos. She had condensed them all into five or six blue binders. We all decided that we would vote first. There were ten not guilty and two guilty. I suggested that the two guilties come forth and see if we could work with them, or if they could work with us to prove to us why some of us said guilty and why some of us said not guilty. No one actually came forward in the beginning. Then #1290 said that she was one of the ones who voted guilty. We never did know who the other guilty vote was, and still don't."

There has been a lot of criticism about how long—or short—the deliberation was. I say, where is it written how long the delib-eration should be? Number one, we were in lockup for eight or nine months. You had nobody you could talk to about the case. Nobody to judge any type of feelings, to answer some of the ques-tions that are on your mind. After the day ended—after you had dinner, after you watched a movie—when you're in that room by yourself at night, you're deliberating with yourself. You're going over what happened in the courtroom. What you felt about it. What questions you have. When they come up the next time, you'll be able to fill in those voids at the next day's session. So it did not take another nine months in that room to deliberate the case, because everybody was going through the same thing. But none of us knew that until we walked into the deliberation room. When we all united, it was just like a cloak had been lifted. We walked into that room and discovered that everybody was in tune to the same thing. That's the reason why it didn't take a long time. The law states that all you need is one reasonable doubt. We had several reasonable doubts, plus the questions we had that never got answered. We went through all the exhibits and the evidence. We did all of that before we reached a verdict.

"There was a question about Mr. Parks' statement concerning whether he saw a 210-pound man go across the driveway and where he really did see him," recalls Marsha. "Well, I distinctly remember that when he was cross-examined, they showed the circle where O.J. supposedly had been standing by Mr. Park. He was standing in his walkway, in that doorway. Not in the driveway. And I wanted to make sure this was understood. When Armanda filled out the paper and we asked for various things, we weren't aware that the judge was going to have the testimony read back. We were thinking that we were going to get the transcript and go through the thing ourselves. The judge told us to wait until one o'clock until the rest of the lawyers got there. When we went back, a lot of the transcript was read. Then there was a break, and we sent a note from the jury room stating that we did not want to hear any more. We had heard the part we wanted to hear. There wasn't any need to listen to the defense's part of the transcript."

Marsha went on. "Since I've been out, I heard Mr. Cochran really got nasty, saying that we should have heard both sides of it. Well, no one knew what we were thinking at that time due to the fact that we were really just going over the evidence and the questions and the doubts that we had in our minds. So if someone had a problem with the time element, we would go back to the time. Let's say that Armanda felt she wanted to know what happened to the little black bag. Or that #247 had a problem with the glove and why was it there. And maybe #2179 had a problem with the glove found at Rockingham, and why there wasn't any blood on the leaves and things of that nature. I had my own thoughts about the glove. Kato had told Fuhrman that he heard loud thumps by the air conditioner. But beyond the air conditioner were cobwebs where no one had ever been. We had walked all through that area during our field trip. We continued to deliberate. We were still throwing things at each other. We were still talking about the doubts and the feelings that each of us had. This is why it took four hours. It was not necessary for us to go over the hundreds and thousands of the evidence pieces and the statements that were made."

"I had a couple of questionable thoughts about Allan Parks," says Carrie. "Allan Parks stated he wasn't sure he could drive his limo into the driveway because there were two cars. But it's a known fact that the other car was not there, that O.J.'s daughter had the other car at the movies. After he got in, it was also a known fact that he could see, from the gate where he was parked, whether someone was coming up the driveway. Marcia Clark is the one who stated, 'Did you see someone in the driveway?' He said, 'I saw a man, a tall, black shadow, someone wearing dark clothes. I don't know whether it was blue or black, walking.' When Cochran questioned Mr. Parks, he asked him where the man was walking, and he traced the path as Mr. Parks answered, and when he ended and circled it, it was in the doorway. The doorway has a long walkway leading out to a bench where O.J. said he was putting his luggage. But when they did let Mr. Parks in, the luggage and the golf bag were out there because Kato stated he also saw O.J. standing in the doorway. And it was simultaneous when Mr. Parks saw them both. One behind the other. Because Kato came around on the side and he was saying he thought O.J. had already let him in. And O.J.'s supposed to have been standing in the door-way. My problem was, Mr. Parks never did say he saw O.J. walking in a specific area on that driveway. He said walkway."

"We went over the evidence. We opened up every binder. We opened up our notebooks. The only thing we all disagreed on was the time in Allan Parks' testimony," Marsha adds. "We all decided that that's what we wanted to hear again. We went over the foot-prints, the crime scene photos, the officers' testimony. A couple of jurors knew a lot of the testimony by heart. A lot of us had to refer to our notes. We went over the pictures. One of the jurors demonstrated that he felt Ron Goldman had connected with somebody, had hit someone's person with his fist, and that's why the bruises were on his hand. We went over in our minds about the glove-fitting demonstration. We went over in our minds that there was one glove at Rockingham and that there was no blood around it. A few jurors truly believed that Detective Fuhrman had planted evidence. There was a lot of discussion about how sloppily the evidence had been handled. How it could have gotten contam-inated. There was a lot of reasonable doubt in that room. There was just no way there could have been a guilty verdict with all the reasonable doubt. It would have been either a hung jury or a not-guilty verdict."

We voiced our opinions and our doubts. The questions came about because we had this ten-to-two vote and we asked what are the subjects that we need to discuss? Right after that, I think it was Carrie who said her main confusion was about Allan Parks, the time element, and whether Allan surely said he saw a black man with a jogging suit. And from that moment, people brought out their Allan Parks notes and verified the time period that he was there and the time period he saw this man and the location. And we pulled out the evidence books and exhibit books and it showed exactly the location where he parked and exactly when he saw that person. So we went through things like that. It took probably about ten minutes of discussion because other people started bringing up other things and other problems and questions they had. And that's when I intervened and said, "Wait a minute. We've got all these issues that we need to discuss," which was Allan Parks' information, information about the glove, information about the EDTA, and information about the puncture wounds and the wounds on Mr. Goldman. Those were the main areas of questioning that we had.

"Wait a minute," I said. "We'll get to all this information, but let's just take one thing at a time." And that's what we did. I asked Carrie to pass out the evidence books.

We asked to hear a readback because there was some conflict. It was my position that anytime there was a conflict in the notes among us, we would request the testimony of that part of the evidence or testimony. And immediately there was conflict with the time of Allan Parks' arrival and the time that he actually saw the person. So I said, "Well, let's request the testimony because I thought that the young lady, the court reporter, would come in and read back that part of the testimony. We had the date. At that time, we heard that the reporters were on call and they would be in in the afternoon. They asked us exactly what part of the testimony we wanted to hear, so we requested that particular section. But when we got into court, Judge Ito indicated that he was going to read all of the testimony of June 28. And after they read the section that we needed to hear and we went on a break, it was not necessary to hear the rest of the testimony. So, the question everyone had was, "Well, Armanda, do you think we have to sit up there and listen to all of it when we've heard everything that we need to hear?" And I said, "You're right. We've heard enough."

One of the other issues was about the bruises on Mr. Goldman's hands. Dave had a problem believing that he actually got those bruises by hitting up against the fence. And then other people would jump in and say, "Yeah, I believe that these came about by him putting up a good struggle, putting up a good fight." But in this case, Dave has studied tae kwon do and he made a few demonstrations for us of how men fight and how they hold their hands. So, certain questions came up about that. We discussed that and reviewed the exhibits and the pictures of that. Everybody had an opportunity. What I did do was go around the table to make sure everybody who may have had a question was able to voice his or her concern. It had nothing to do with whether or not you believed O.J. was guilty or not guilty. It's just to clear out a lot of things that may have been on your mind.

Sheila had a question regarding EDTA on the fence. Other people jumped in. It was amazing that we were all thinking the same thing and all had some of the same questions. The notes were basically all consistent. We pulled up the exhibits. This is how we did our discussion.

"One juror, #1233, asked, Why was there EDTA in the blood on the fence and why wasn't there EDTA in the blood trails at Bundy?" Marsha notes. "We also discussed the glove found at Bundy. If it was on Mr. Simpson's hand, how did the glove get off Mr. Simpson's hand? How could Mr. Goldman pull the glove off Mr. Simpson's hand and not turn the glove inside out? How did the glove just slip off Mr. Simpson's hand? While I do truly believe that the glove fit Mr. Simpson's hand, I feel it was a tight fit. That was one of my doubts. How did Mr. Simpson get cut in this fight if he had the knife? That was another one of my doubts. That he cut his own hand. The cut he had on his hands didn't look like a cut from a knife fight to me. The time element to me was a big factor. The prosecution didn't prove to me that Mr. Simpson could have done all of this damage in this time frame."

One thing I would like to get straight was that Fuhrman was not the main reason we came to our decision. And I'm so glad he did not come into our conversation until toward the end of our deliberation. I think a lot of hostility would have set in early on based on the fact that he denied he ever used the n-word, that type of thing. Remember, we never got the opportunity to hear all of the tapes, we just heard certain segments. But Fuhrman did not come up until the end. And when he came up, I think Juror #1290 said, "Well, we know he's a liar. So we don't even have to deal with that." Certain other comments came up about him, but other than that, he never even came up as part of our reasoning. He was not one of the reasonable doubts as far as we're concerned.

One of the other questions several people had was about the EDTA that was found on the gate being consistent with Mr. Simpson's blood, and the DNA in that particular blood sample being higher than any of the others that had been taken or collected. Everybody went back to their notes and compared whatever they had about the information. But once we looked at everything, we still could not come up with the understanding of how, after coming back a week or so later to collect this blood, it had not degraded. That was one of the issues. Another was the glove found at Rockingham. Supposedly someone had come down the pathway along the side of the house, hit the side of the air conditioner, and made this noise that Kato heard, and dropped the glove. The question was, if the person—Mr. Simpson is about six feet—if he dropped the glove and it was so bloody, why wasn't there blood on anything else? If the glove hits the ground, surely some blood would stick to the leaves. We checked the notes and went over that.

No matter what anybody thinks, we paid close attention throughout the trial. We all had extensive notes and were all thinking along the same lines when it came down to the deliberation. Still, I think boredom became a factor during some of the testimony from the expert witnesses. When they tried so hard to explain things to you, it almost seemed like they thought they were dealing with a bunch of illiterate, ignorant people. After a while, when you're hearing something repeated over and over, you probably do get a bored look. Even Judge Ito would be yawning and going off the deep end sometimes. Especially when it came down to the DNA experts. I mean, that stuff was thrown at us day after day after day. You just got there and you said, "Damn. Are they going to ever stop?" For instance, Dr. Cotton. I'm sure she's outstanding in her field. I have no doubt about that. We had no problem with any of that evidence whatsoever. We thought it was presented superbly. Gary Sims, outstanding witness. But I think they just overdosed us on it and we just shut down after a while. But the bottom line is, these people could test only what was given to them. If they're given bad evidence from jump street, you're going to get some degraded answers and responses. But we had no problem with their presentation. We all understood. That was one of the questions. Do you have any problem with the DNA? Do we need to get this explained? Do you understand this? The answer was no. We know about these autorads. We know about aliels, gels, we know all of that. A lot of us felt we could now earn a medical degree. Naturally, there would be days on which we would be bored. I'm sure Judge Ito recognized this, and he'd call for comfort breaks in between so we could rest.

I think part of the problem for the prosecution was the way a good deal of the evidence was handled. I think that L.A. County, a county as big as we have, needs to update its equipment and train its employees properly. The fact is, the county has gotten into a situation where they try to do more for less and the end result you get when you try to push a heavy workload on people is that they make mistakes. But it comes down to a point in this particular case where Dr. Golden had made thirty errors in the autopsy. Now, you can't tell me that this man has not made errors on previous autopsies. And that comes about through rushing, trying to complete your assignment to keep up with the workload. But this just happened to be a case that came to court as a "high-profile" case and the problems were brought to everyone's attention.

I think we need to allocate the funds in certain areas so that in these types of situations you get good evidence that's preserved properly, that all the checks and stuff are run on top-of-the-line equipment. I'm just as guilty as the next person when it comes to talking about raising taxes. I'm the first one to vote no because you don't want this money coming out of your pocket. But it's time we started voting yes on some of these issues and started allocating funds so that the county can get proper equipment, good employees, updated procedure manuals. It is ridiculous to run a department when you don't have a procedure manual. You know, they've been working on a procedure manual for five years or however long it was. That makes no sense to me at all. And Dennis Fung just got caught up in a situation where that was how they've been working. They've been doing it like this ever since he was employed, so how would he know any different? This is just how it has happened. Nothing has changed. So he thought that whatever he was doing in his collection procedures and his handling of the evidence was done properly. Because when they threw the collection of that evidence in that van, in that criminalist's truck in the midday, hot as it was, nonrefrigerated, what was going to happen to those swatches, to that evidence? It's going to degrade. It has to. Something has to happen. These are things that have been going on all along, I'm sure. Naturally, all these different errors and stuff are going to come out, and we are in a position where we have to reach a decision based on the evidence that is presented to us. That's what people have to remember: We had to judge the evidence we were presented with within the rules of the law.

We reviewed every question that came up. No one was excluded and no issue was overlooked. Then, as we got about three hours into it, I don't know which one, but one of the jurors said, "Ladies and gentlemen, what do we have here?" And it came up, well, what we really have here is reasonable doubt. At that point , which was before we had the readback, we took another vote to see where we were. It was also a secret vote. This time, we all made the same choice. I went around to each and every person just to make sure that he or she was satisfied. You know, you've got to live with yourself. That's my main thing. But everybody was sure. We had put in the verdict and then we filled out these forms that the court sends you. As a matter of fact, we had to wait for those.

I think I made the statement, "God, this was a little too easy here." What I had heard about deliberations was that people are at each other's throats. And I think Yolanda Crawford said no jury she has ever been on has run as smoothly. And Ann, who has been on eight juries, said the same thing. People don't realize when you live with people for a long period of time you can almost predetermine what their thoughts are, what their feelings are. One night during the trial I looked around and thought, *What the hell am I doing here with these people? Why did my number have to come up out of all these thousands of people?* I believe that fate hands you certain situations at certain times for a certain reason, but for the life of me I couldn't figure out why. Then it dawned on me. I looked around and I figured one reason is, nobody's a quitter. No matter how much we complained, day after day we still hung in there. We still tried to maintain the respect and the order the court had given us about not doing certain things. And we hung in there. I don't care if we went into our rooms and started screaming and hollering. We'd still get up the next day and go down to that courtroom and be very attentive. We were all fighters in that respect.

In the end, when we got into that room, everybody was on the same wavelength. I don't know if it would have been the same if Willie or Calhoun were in there voting—they both have dominant personalities and like to get their points across—but I'm sure we would have worked it out. As it was, everybody had the same questions, the same ideas, and it just ran so smoothly. We did not raise our voices. I mean, there came a time when I had to say, "Calm down. Let's take these one at a time. Everybody can't talk at the same time." But you're so excited at that moment. You're talking. Everybody is talking. It's just amazing. It's an amazing feeling to realize that after all this time, people are thinking the same way I'm thinking. Now, maybe if it had come down to where we were in total disagreement, then we would have experienced something entirely different. But that didn't happen. And when we took our second vote, we had a unanimous verdict: not guilty on both counts.

10

A Reasonable Doubt

===

O.J. Simpson may be acquitted, but the public and the media will never quit. O.J. will never rest easy again. Wherever he goes, he will never be the O.J. that he was before. What he gets, he will have to work to get it. Before, it was easy. You could mingle and run around. But I do believe it will never be as easy as it was before for him—that's all in the past.

—ARMANDA COOLEY

October 2, 1995

After we had deliberated and had come up with a verdict, you could see the looks of happiness on our faces. We were thinking, *We finally get to go home. It's over. Oh, my God.* But then the tears came. Not because of the sense of relief or happiness, but because we felt so bad for the Brown and Goldman families. We started hugging each other and crying. We felt so bad for the families.

As the foreman, I used the same management skills I use in

167

my job. I am basically a very good people-oriented person. I deal with people very well. I went to each and every juror and reconfirmed the verdict. I asked them, "Are you going to be able to sleep tonight? Is there something on your mind that we need to stop and discuss that will help you know that you have made the right decision?" Then I asked myself the same thing. My answer was, "I will have no trouble sleeping tonight."

Based on the job they gave me to do and the equipment they gave me, which was the law, I really believe we did a hell of a job. That's how we dealt with accepting our decision. Because if you allow yourself to get wrapped up in saying over and over, "God, did I do the right thing? Well, what if they were right and he did change his clothes?," you'll start going through all these ifs and what abouts, and you'll drive yourself stone crazy.

"Right after we took the final vote," Marsha explains, "Armanda informed the court that we had a verdict. She filled out the forms the court had given us and put them back in the folder. The deputy came in and gave her a manila envelope. Armanda put the papers inside the folder and put the folder inside the manila envelope and sealed it. They deputy put tape across the seal and she signed the tape. Then we went back into court and Judge Ito excused us until the verdict would be read on Tuesday morning."

That night, everyone knew that we would be leaving the following day and the hotel staff was kind enough to give us a big dinner out on the balcony. The chefs were out there barbequeing steaks. The hotel provided us with a steak dinner and supplied drinks and live music—something a little bit different than we had been accustomed to. I really enjoyed it, but I didn't understand why we couldn't have gotten that same type of treatment during the whole nine months we were there.

"The hotel had organized what's known as the last supper for the jurors," adds Marsha. "Right around seven o'clock, we were all invited up to this really nice suite and there was a jazz pianist there. They provided cocktails for us—beer and wine, hors d'oeuvres. The fourteen jurors were there, a few deputies, some of the hotel staff, and also the hotel manager. We laughed and joked, drank and ate. From the beginning of the trial to the end, Carrie used to sing and whistle 'Misty' and the pianist played that song for her."

"It was marvelous," Carrie remembers. "We went up to the nineteenth floor, where we got a chance to meet the hotel's general manager, Louis N. Feder. We also got a chance to meet the staff of the laundry department, the housekeeping people, and the other members of the hotel staff. When we came back from court that afternoon, we asked Sergeant Smith, 'Since this is our last day, can we have a beer or a bottle of wine or something?' Even though we had made a decision, we all were tense, a little on edge. So he said, 'Of course, I'll look into that for you.' And about four-thirty he told us, 'The hotel is planning something for us. We're going to go upstairs about seven o'clock. We're going to have a few cocktails and then we're going to have dinner about eight o'clock.' It was so nice. We went upstairs and, after living on the fifth floor for nine months, it was like a whole new hotel. This place was absolutely gorgeous. It was like a whole apartment up there. They had everything set up for us. We had the finest of wines. We had beer. We had champagne. Drinks had been something once in a blue moon. Maybe a beer or two. They were very cautious about our indulgence and I'm very thankful for that. The limit was two per person. We had a pianist who played at the Inter-Continental Hotel in the evenings. I sat on the barstool in front of the piano with my glass of champagne, and she asked what I would like to hear. She played 'Misty' and I tried to sing along with it. Then a couple more of the young ladies and Dave gathered around the piano and we started singing. Then she started playing different music. We were dancing a little bit, socializing with the staff. We were all happy. We knew we were having our last supper together as the O.J. Simpson jurors. The atmosphere at the party was magnificent. There was a bunch of hair letting-down, a lot of dancing, and two or three hee-haws that let us know we had finally made our decision and come to the end of our long journey."

Remarks Marsha, "We stayed up there about an hour or hour and a half before going back downstairs to the fourth floor, where they set up dinner in our regular buffet room. But this time they put in long tables and they made it a little more elegant for us. Outside, on the terrace off the buffet room, there were two chefs cooking steaks. There were also different types of salads set up outside. Everyone really relaxed. We were all having our cocktails and talking about what we would do when we got home, where we were going to go. It was a nice evening, a calm evening. It was beautiful outside."

On Tuesday morning, everyone was a little nervous. There were a lot of mixed emotions, but no one said much to each other except good morning. It seemed like we were lost in our own thoughts. I had called my girlfriend Carol to tell her to pick me and Marsha up after the verdicts were read. I had arranged for her to make reservations for us to fly to Vegas. We were busy getting our things together, getting our bags on the cart to move them downstairs to the vans. The only thing we noticed that was different was that there were a lot of extra deputies around. But people were just busy hustling and bustling, getting ready to go. There was a lot of activity on the floor, but not much talk other than small comments like, "Girl, I'll be glad to get home."

"I woke up that morning, and my stomach was sort of upset. It was kind of tight. I was scared. I was nervous. I was excited. I was emotional," says Marsha. "I felt like I was leaving my new friends, my new family. My stomach was tied up in a knot. My breathing was erratic. I felt like I was going to hyperventilate. I didn't know how I was going to react when the verdict was read. I really don't recall what I actually was thinking that morning. I felt excited that I was getting ready to go home. I thought, *Damn, I'm actually going home.* But I knew I couldn't go home right away because I'd been advised not to go there for a couple of days due to all the media. The deputies had called my mother the evening before because we were no longer able to talk to anyone over the phone. So the deputies talked for us. We'd tell the deputies what to ask. They asked my mother what was going on there. She informed me that all types of media were calling and that they were gathering in front of the house. I told her that I wouldn't be coming there right away, that I would get in touch with her and tell her what I wanted her to do about meeting me at the airport."

"I awoke early that morning. We normally had to get up at six-thirty, but I was up at six due to the fact that we had to pack all of our things and make sure everything was out of the hotel room before we left," says Carrie. "The only thing I was thinking was, *Oh, my God, we're going to read the verdict.* We're going to be finished. We're going to get a chance to go home to our families. We're going to be able to go to the bathroom by ourselves. We're not going to have to watch the TV that they show us. We'll be able to drive our cars. We'll be able to dial our telephones. Just do the things that we normally do. All of us. We would walk the halls and say small things to each other like, 'Thank God it's over.'"

The first part of the ride to the courthouse was routine. It was sort of exciting in a scary way. There were all those cops and we could see that several streets were blocked off. We saw mounted police. We saw a lot of police cars with riot gear inside and there seemed to be a million helicopters in the sky. There were also a lot of people out in front of the courthouse. You couldn't see them, but you could definitely hear them. On our way to the courthouse, we pulled up beside a newsstand and I was able to look at the front page and the headline said RUSH TO JUDGMENT. I still remember that. I didn't mention it to anyone because I didn't know what it really meant at the time. I didn't know if it meant we, the jurors, had rushed to judgment or that the prosecution had rushed to judgment, because the defense had often said that during the trial.

"We left a little late that morning. Normally, we would leave about seven forty-five, but we left about eight. The ride to the courthouse was not the normal ride," recalls Carrie. "We usually went down to Third and came across and made two turns. This time, we went around a block or two. In our course of going there, we noticed right away there was something out of the norm. There were a lot of police cars. There was riot gear in the cars. We could see more media. We could see a lot of people. We were so nervous. 'Oh, my God, what's going to happen?' we were saying. 'I just pray to God we can get out of this. I just hope everything goes smoothly.' Marsha, Armanda, Sheila, Mr. Calhoun, Bea, Yolanda, and I all rode in the same van. We were just tense. We looked at each other. Armanda said, 'Oh, it's going to be all right. All we have to do is just get in there and do our job.' The others said, 'Our day has come. This is the big day.' It was the most amazing thing. I remember the time when we went out to O.J. Simpson's house and we had the caravan and the seven or eight helicopters and all the police cars. This was totally different from that. This time it was more of a still, a quiet. It was an eerie feeling. The atmosphere was strange. It was noisy outside—there were people lined up on the street—but you never heard anything. I could not hear the people, but I could see the looks on the their faces. They were amazed."

Beyond all the activity in the streets, the only thing outside the norm was that we had extra deputies. There was a deputy on either end of us as we filed into the courtroom to have the verdict read. It was a strange feeling because when I walked out, basically I was the last one at the end of the line because of where I sat, and as soon as you hit that door you see all these faces, and they really had a different look than they ordinarily had. It seemed like thousands of people were crowded in there to hear the verdict. At one point, I was getting so paranoid because all I could see were heads—no bodies. It seemed like all these heads were just bunched together. Immediately I thought, *Oh my God, I can't be looking at these people*, and that's the reason I sort of directed my vision toward the judge and toward Deirdre Robertson. But it just felt like the people were right on top of us in the jury box.

Marsha agrees. "To me, it looked like there were a million people in that little cramped-up space. I don't know if it was really that many, or many more than were normally there, but it seemed like it was standing room only. And it felt like everybody was just staring right at me, looking me right in my face, right in my mouth, just looking right at me. So I just refused to look at anyone. I just sat there. But I can tell you I could see my shirt moving. My heart was pounding and my hands started to get cold. I was actually starting to hyperventilate and I was sitting there and I whispered, 'Lord.' And then when I found out we were each going to be questioned after they read the verdict, I got really nervous because I didn't know that, I just thought that once she read it that was it. So I kept telling myself, just calm down. I was trying to keep on my mind that the man's name was Orenthal and not to twist that up. So I just kept trying to think, because I always thought that the foreman read the verdict, I didn't know but then when the judge had said the clerk would read the verdict. It was like, I just wanted to say, ssshh, you know, I was just really truly relieved at that particular point. I was feeling total relief. But still just focusing on the judge and focusing on Mrs. Robertson when she read. I didn't look at the defense, I didn't look at the prosecution, I didn't even look at the people at that point. I just stayed focused on the judge and Mrs. Robertson."

Judge Ito already had the sealed verdict from Monday—the envelope with the tape and my name on it. The court clerk had passed it to the judge and the judge had one of the sheriffs give it to me, and he said, "Madam Foreman, are these your initials?"

And I said yes, and then I had to open it up and I couldn't get that damn thing open to save my life. I fumbled with it for what seemed like five minutes and then I could see Judge Ito holding a knife. "Oh, he's got a big knife. He got a knife, oh he got a hell of a knife, he got a knife," says Carrie. "I don't know if he keeps it at his desk, but he got a big knife.") The deputy was going to pass the knife over to me but by that time I managed to get the tape off. I passed the envelope back to him and Judge Ito went through the papers and he asked me, "Are these papers in order?" and I said yes. And he looked through the papers, just reviewing what we had written on them. That's when I noticed he had an unpleasant look about him.

"I knew something was funny when he read it, because I could see his color change. I definitely saw the expression on his face change," notes Carrie.

Then the judge asked Mr. Simpson to stand and face us while Mrs. Robertson read the verdict. I thought, *Well, this is it*, and I looked right at him as he turned toward us. The man can't look at everybody at the same time, but somehow I felt like he was looking right at me. And you are trying not to be nervous, you're trying to look straight ahead, but I couldn't help feeling that he was looking directly at me.

"Yeah, I sort of felt that way, too, because the only time I looked at him was when the judge said, 'Would you stand and face the jurors,' and he was looking at us," adds Marsha. "I didn't look at him. I didn't look at any of them. And I kept telling myself to remember what it was like when we would go to church and the pastor would say, 'Relax and breathe and praise God.' And so I kept whispering, 'Praise God,' over and over and kept trying to regulate my breathing. Because my hands were getting cold, and I felt like I was about to pass out. But then she started to read the verdict and she couldn't get his name quite right. She stumbled over pronouncing Orenthal. She was nervous, but I would have been, too, if I had to read it. I'm just glad I didn't."

At first, I was thinking she stumbled because maybe she was upset by it. And then you say, well, maybe she's just nervous. And you're still not trying to show any emotion or anything. But she read it and then . . .

Says Carrie, "Oh man, you could see the people looking, and you could hear a big old wave of 'AAAHHH,' and then I could hear her—I could hear her just screaming out—Ron Goldman's sister, just screaming. And I could hear 'WHOOOO,' you know, it's like you couldn't hear what they were saying, but there was mumbling and it was like a big rolling wave of sound coming at you. And you could hear all this hollering. And all I wanted to do was get out of there."

"I heard that and I felt a cracking down on my rear end because I really felt I was about to have diarrhea sitting there," recalls Marsha. "I'm saying, 'Oh, Lord, oh Jesus, just hurry up and get me out of here. As a matter of fact, I sort of sat on my hands because I felt I was about to move. It was just a lot of pressure."

At that point I had stopped looking. I couldn't look anymore. I was just trying to hold on. I just wanted him to take the gavel and say, "Order in the court," but he didn't.

"O.J. put his hand up like this and waved to us," adds Carrie, raising her hand. "And then I looked at Marcia Clark, I looked at the prosecution, and they looked like 'You mother . . . ,' you know what I'm saying. All I can hear is this girl just screaming."

"And I said, 'Oh, Jesus,' because I was about to cry, too. I'm about to cry and fill myself up, too. You've heard of cases where people's body functions are just totally let down," says Marsha. "I felt so sad for the people that truly believed justice wasn't served. I felt sad for the Goldman family. I felt sad for the Brown family. I could hear the Simpson family start crying, or some type of emotion coming from the Simpson side. Out of the corner of my eye, I could see Ms. Clark and Mr. Darden look down. Solemn looks on their faces. I had all this to deal with and all I wanted to do at that point was just get up and walk out."

After the verdict was read, I didn't hear a thing. It was like numb city. I know we were polled about our decision, but I don't remember what the man said after everybody had said yes, your honor, that is my verdict. I don't know what happened next. All I can remember is being excused, and then the judge saying something about taking care of some business with the lawyers. We started crying before we could get out of the room.

"When we got out there, everybody was just crying," Carrie says. "And Sheila Woods, #8, she was crying loud, that girl was going off."

We were consoling each other, saying, "We did what we had to do." It was just terrible. I truly believe it was just a cry of relief, of the stress being relieved, of being able to go home now. I knew people were going to miss each other, but there was so much built up inside us, we had no other way to release it except to cry. We hugged each other, said our good-byes, exchanged numbers.

"Well, once we got back in the room, I couldn't sit down. I was constantly walking back and forth to the window," says Carrie. "And it looked like the people outside were just swelling. Every time I looked, there were more and more people and I just kept saying, 'Oh my God, are they going to riot, are they going to get us?' I really was scared and frightened. The reason I was so frightened was because I felt the verdict we had reached was going to anger a lot of people. I had no idea it would touch sparks all the way to the White House. I had no idea President Clinton would have spoken about it. We tried to make conversation in that room but nobody really wanted to. Everybody was just walking around each other, looking out the windows, wondering what was coming next."

"It was scary as hell," Marsha emphasizes. "You know how you see courtroom dramas and the wrong verdict comes down, or somebody thinks the verdict is wrong, and somebody jumps up and starts shooting or something? We didn't know what was happening."

After the verdict was read and we went back to the deliberation room, emotions were running high. Some people hugged, some cried because they felt so bad for the families of the people who were murdered. That's when Ann came over and said to me, "In spite of it all, I still feel he's guilty. But the evidence just was not there and I had no other choice. He did it, they just screwed up on the evidence." I knew she had questions. I think at the time of the first vote—when she had given her guilty verdict—she stood up and said, "I'm the one who gave the guilty verdict," but I have no idea who the other person was because he or she never spoke up. And I did not force the issue at the time. In the end, after the last vote, I just wanted to make sure that everybody was satisfied with the verdict. Obviously, there was one other person who had a doubt at the time. In order for that person to have changed his or her vote to not guilty, it would had to have been from one of the ten discussions we had during deliberation. If the person really believed there was a reason why he was guilty, he or she never voiced what it was.

I know the majority of the dismissed jurors also agreed with our decision based on the evidence they heard, but I think it's interesting that they also were aware of the additional information that was kept from us, that Mark Fuhrman had taken the fifth, for example. I learned that Jeanette Harris and Willie Cravin would have also voted not guilty. "The prosecution did not prove its case beyond a reasonable doubt," Harris says. "The evidence was just too questionable."

"There were several things I took into consideration," Cravin explains. "There was EDTA, the substance that they found on the back gate that was in the blood, so I wanted to know how was it possible that this could be found in the blood that was found on the back gate when this is something that is used to prevent blood clotting and this is supposed to be in the blood vial in the lab. If this is not coming out of your regular bloodstream, then how did it appear on the back gate? Then I wondered why they were col-

lecting blood evidence in July when the crime scene was closed in
June. Which means that everyone in the world could come
through there, so why are we going back collecting evidence when
thousands of people could tramp through there just because they
wanted to see Nicole's house?

"I felt that if Mr. Simpson had killed these people, there should
have been a lot of blood, I mean, a tremendous amount of blood
leaving from the crime scene out to the alley where he was supposed to have gotten into the Bronco, and then there would be a
lot of blood on the Bronco, not one or two drops but a tremendous
amount of blood. There were the two theories about him going
over the fence and then hitting the wall near Kato Kaelin's room,
the three thumps that were supposed to be him going over the
wall, and the other theory where he got out of the Bronco and
there were blood drops on the driveway up to the foyer. Now these
are just drops, so I would think they would have one theory rather
than two and then try to pursue that one theory rather then saying, well, he went over the wall, but there was no blood found on
the wall, there was no blood on the house, there was no blood
where the glove was found. The carpets were swiped, so if there
was blood leading up to the carpet, why wasn't there blood leading
from the carpet going upstairs? And he had to wash up, so why
wasn't there blood in the drain? They say he had taken a shower.
They checked the drain. There was no blood in the shower. There
was no blood in the drain, so there were too many things.

"And this is the only trial I've ever heard of in my life where a
prosecution witness takes the fifth," Cravin continues. "Usually
it's the defense, the guy doesn't want to testify because he's going
to incriminate himself. Instead, it's Mark Fuhrman, a prosecution
witness who was supposed to help convict the defendant, and he
comes up and takes the fifth. And then the coroner, the one who
performed the autopsy, isn't allowed to testify. Usually the coroner's the one you want to hear because he's going to solidify your
foundations as far as the defendant is concerned. They didn't want

the coroner, Golden, to testify because he had made so many mistakes. Then Dr. Lakshamanan comes on and it takes him eight days to testify, and he wasn't even the one who performed the autopsy."

11

THE RACE CARD

Anytime there is a racist problem, this country is split. That is a bad problem. That's like Russia, Red China, North Africa, South Africa. We got the same thing. This black and white America. Black and white . . .

—CARRIE BESS

After the trial was finally over and we had returned from our trip to Las Vegas, we began to hear a lot about racism and the verdict. We were stunned because race didn't occur to us when we were deliberating on whether O.J. was or was not guilty of murder. What did occur to me and the others was the tragedy involved. It's a tragic case and I still feel sorry for the people who lost loved ones. I truly do. We just did what we had to do. We just worked with what they gave us and never put any more thought to it than that. It was a murder case. There was a man on trial who was accused of murdering two people. Naturally, during the prosecution's examination of their witnesses, I thought O.J. was guilty. When they were cross-examined, I would try to make up little scenarios and try to picture them. When I was lying in bed at night, I would try to picture how this could have happened. While I was sitting in the courtroom, I tried to imagine

181

the scenarios. It was like watching a movie. In the end, we made a decision that he was not guilty, but I think it is important to remember that we have not declared him innocent at all. Myself and others such as Michael Knox truly believe that he knew something about it.

Jeanette Harris summarized our predicament nicely when she said that race could have played a part in the verdict, but the evidence was so questionable that no one had to use the race card to come to this verdict. "I believe that after being there, we were taken out of reality and racial issues along normal lines. After a month, we were no longer ourselves because we were so saturated with the legal things. I think the jury delivered a verdict based on the lack of evidence and the shoddy case the prosecution presented," she explains.

For all the time we were sequestered, we heard very little about racial stuff. I guess that's the reason why everybody on the jury, and I say everybody, was shocked when we learned racism was so heavily involved in people's reactions after the trial. Racism is here and it's been here for ages, but the fact that this trial was used to emphasize it even more by accusing us of being racists is what's appalling to me. After all that time, 267 days, we walk out of the Trial of the Century and are accused of being racists. We are accused of letting O.J. Simpson get away with murder because he is the same skin color as we are.

Remember, we had been underground and had no idea this was going to happen. When we found out, we all felt this strange, numb feeling. You could say we were shocked, or you could say we were outraged, that people would even think of us sitting there making decisions based on race. And it proved to me that they felt that we had no intelligence whatsoever. I'm still shocked. I hate to even listen to the news, different talk programs, because this is what we're constantly hearing every day. On the one hand, sometimes I am so angry that I just want to jump out there and say something or do something to try to protect myself or try to make a point. And then, on the other hand, I want to run away and hide because I don't know exactly what drove people to feel this. Each day I'm out, each moment I'm out—and I say *out* because it's like we were moles living underneath the ground—each day we're out, we hear more and more things we never had the opportunity to hear in the trial. It's as if a whole second trial went on with another jury.

It's important that people know this was not a racist thing. I'm black and Mr. Simpson is black. However, Mr. Simpson lives in a white world. When we signed up to do our civic duty, it was People versus Orenthal J. Simpson, not People versus Racism or People versus the Politicians or People versus Battered Women and Children. I'm just as sensitive to racism as the next person is, but people need to know that was not our cause whatsoever. I don't care what color Mr. Simpson is. If the evidence had been there to find him guilty, then that's what I would have done.

"Once we got out, the media were incredible," Marsha remarks. "On the news we're hearing that 60 percent of the people are saying this was a verdict based on racism. You also hear the president of the United States saying that the United States has been split as far as racism is concerned. And another thing, they also pretend like racism never existed in this country, that throughout the years we managed to get rid of it and then all of a sudden based on our verdict in the jury, we brought it back. I beg to differ. When I walked into that courtroom I did not think about racism. I hadn't given it any racial thought even prior to going in to the decision. I hadn't put any type of race thing to it at all. And I still don't. I was watching CNN's 'Talk Back Live,' one of those talk shows. Dick Gregory was on there and he was talking about the Million Man March and every other person is talking about this verdict and how it is dividing up everybody. This is not because of the verdict. All of this was in place before we came on the scene. It's amazing that suddenly all of this is welling up because it certainly didn't start with the O.J. Simpson case."

"I don't understand how people could say that I let someone go because he was black," Marsha continues. "If I hadn't been on the trial and O.J. had been my relative and it was proven to me that he had killed these two people, he'd be in prison. I don't care who he is or what color he is. People don't know me. They've passed judgment on me. You tell the world I created this big division. The division was there before I was even part of the jury. I have never even been part of any type of division. It angers me. It really angers me for people to say that because I was a black woman, I let this black man go. If they had proven to me that this black man had killed two people, that black man would be in prison. Simple as that."

What do people want? I asked myself. *Forty acres and a mule, sweetheart.* Everybody needs to know that the racial cards that were played in the actual courtroom were not played or by any means used in the deliberation room. It wasn't racist going in. It wasn't a racist case. If that were the case, we could have been angry at O.J. for being with a white woman. It could be either way. We didn't even see racism in this. But think about it. Being black women, we could have been angry as heck at O.J. for going with a white woman. But that wasn't the case.

We have heard that to most people, O.J. was like a white guy. That's why this has become so amazing. They say we let him off because he was famous and had charm.

"Charm?" questions Marsha. "Well, that's what they say. But I never met him. I'm nobody's groupie. Nobody impresses me that much. I like to watch old movies. Old black and whites. My favorite actress is Katharine Hepburn. I love her. I love 'I Love Lucy.' I lived on the big island of Hawaii in 1975. You see a lot of stars coming through there because I worked for airport security. When they're on vacation, they're just like anybody else. I'm no star chaser. When you play football, that's a job. You make good money doing what you want to do. You're comfortable. I carry mail. I'm happy with my life. They say, 'Oh, he's a big star and he could afford all these lawyers and that's why he got off.' Well, that wasn't the case with me. If they had proven to me that he had done it, I would have found him guilty."

The issue that has really bothered us about these accusations is we know about racism. We as African-American women have lived in a racist society for a very long time. "As I was growing up, I was called a nigger a lot of times," says Carrie. "I've gone places where they wouldn't serve me. I went through Mississippi where they would only serve me through the side window. I was working at this one place and they didn't even allow me to come in the front door. I know what it's like. But I also know black people who are married to white people. We have raised different kids in our family. This is life. You learn. You know it's there. There are so many people who don't know it's there. It doesn't mean you have to be bitter, but you know it's there. When you see it, you know how to get around it unless someone pushes you to the wall and you have to react. But I know it's there. And I will always know it's there.

"It's a lot better now because at least there's no sign that says 'Colored,'" Carrie continues. "We can go downtown and we can go in any store now. When I was growing up, you couldn't do that. We couldn't go in those stores. I remember the man walking up to collect the rent from my grandmother and saying 'Lewis, where them nigger boys? Lewis, where them nigger girls?' It was just flat out. It wasn't no biting, no bullets, no anything. It was just something they used. Where I went to school, it was all black kids. It wasn't integrated. You can rest assured that I've seen my day. We couldn't play basketball with them. The only thing we could do with the whites was noncontact sports. We could run track. We couldn't play football. We couldn't play basketball. We couldn't play anything where you touch. We had a marching band. Our band was the greatest band. We traveled all over Missouri. Cape

Girardeau and all the places. When they integrated, they took all the best people from that school. They wouldn't take everybody. Not everyone could go. They chose the cream of the crop."

We all agree L.A. is better for us versus living in the South, but racism is still here. You just have to know and be aware of what's going on. You're not looking for it but if it happens, you know it's there. I used to work at CBS when they were taping "Soul Train." There came a time when you wanted to say things but you couldn't. You have to be careful what you say because people do not take it lightly. If I came up and complained about a couple of black kids who were doing wrong, it's okay. But you couldn't just say that these two kids did wrong and they happened to be white. If you're black, you couldn't do that. You just have to be careful. It's still the same. I feel it will be that way forever, as long as we feel that we cannot speak out. I feel that we should be able to speak on wrong regardless of what side it is. Let's also understand that there are racist blacks. There are racist whites. There are racists within racists, and it's not as if we didn't see racism during the trial. We did, but we did not consider it in our deliberations. I don't care if you're black, white, or whatever the situation may be. You mean all the black people are saying that he's not guilty because he's black? Because he's black you mean to tell me that he can't murder anybody? He can't kill anybody? Only white people can kill people or Hispanics or whatever? That is not true. People just need to be accountable for what they say and what they believe.

People are saying that Johnnie Cochran played the race card right from the start. I didn't pick up on that at all. I know he just kept saying in his opening statement, "Pay attention to Detective Fuhrman. He's the only one who found all the evidence." I didn't pick up that Fuhrman was a racist. I just picked up that Fuhrman was lying. He was a liar. I didn't ever put any type of racism to that. So I don't know if that's being naive or if that's just how I perceived it. I didn't see that Cochran was trying to put any type of racism on that.

"Johnnie played a race card, but he's a criminal lawyer," Carrie contends. "He's supposed to play every card in the deck to get his client off. That's the law. I am surprised that the prosecuting attorneys let it go so far knowing that they had a problem with Fuhrman as opposed to bringing it out to us. I think it would have been a much different situation because we had an opportunity to throw out all or any part of Fuhrman's testimony. And Fuhrman was the trial. Fuhrman found the hat. Fuhrman found the glove. Fuhrman found the blood. Fuhrman went over the gate. Fuhrman did everything. When you throw it out, what case do you have? You've got reasonable doubt right there before you even get to the criminalists. Why didn't the prosecuting attorneys know that they had built their case on what Fuhrman had said along with Vannatter? Why didn't they protect themselves by clarifying that Fuhrman situation as opposed to him taking the fifth and just leaving them holding the bag?

"It would have been a lot different," Carrie continues. "To me, it was like something being hidden and you were covering for him. You knew this was a problem and Johnnie Cochran let it go all the way down to the wire. He let you play your cards all the way down to the wire and then he said the part about sending a message to the L.A.P.D. Well, I'll tell you how I took that. I did not take it as, we're not going to let the whole L.A.P.D. get away with this. It's that we realize there is trouble in the L.A.P.D. force. There are people out there. There are more Fuhrmans than we saw. This is the time to do what you've gotta do. Well, it was obvious to me already what I had to do. When we got the chance to listen to those tapes, the judge told us, 'You have a right to discredit all or any parts of his testimony.' "

In the case of the trial, racism was the furthest thing from our minds. What we were concerned about was one of the alternate jurors, who definitely seemed racist.

"Armanda went to the point where she said that it was a worry," Marsha remembers. "With the jurors dropping like flies, he was an alternate, and could actually be sitting in there, and he did have attitudes. She said, 'I would have gone as far as, if he actually had been selected, writing a letter saying that we had a problem with this man.'"

"Mr. Calhoun let it be known," Carrie adds. "He spoke on it. He would argue a point. He would blurt it out. It wasn't something he tried to hide. And I'm quite sure if he was asked before God and anybody else, I don't think he'd hide it again. He'd get mad at us because we socialized with whites. It's a fact."

"What was so weird about Mr. Calhoun," Marsha says, "and I'll tell you something. I really liked that man. I still don't have any problems with Mr. Calhoun. I just think he was a man who was raised in the South. I never had any problem with racism or anything. If I put all my family in here. My grandfather's white. My mother's father. You would not believe the array of people I have in my family. Color is not an issue. I was the one who started calling him Mr. Calhoun. Beatrice was the same age as him and we called her Bea. So, I gave him that title. That's what I called him. Maybe everybody else picked it up, too, because he was a preacher and my grandfather on my father's side was a preacher. Just out of total respect. I could make him laugh. He sat at the table one day. He started laughing so hard, he started choking. We joked. I knew he really didn't care for white people. I didn't find that out until later on. He is a racist. He didn't like my brother David at all. Until the day we left, David didn't give that man anything but total respect. He had a thing about David. He would tolerate him. I don't know if David caught it at all. I never said a word. We were sitting at the table one day and Jeanette told us she had a twin sister who died. I couldn't believe it. Mr. Calhoun,

Tracy, Michael, myself, Bess, Armanda, Sheila, and her. We were talking about family. I think that was when I came back from the first funeral. Mr. Calhoun said, 'Well, when it's your time to go, it's your time to go.' I looked around and I said to myself, 'Well, I'm going to leave that alone. I'm not going to say anything.' This is the preacher. We had two deaths at the same time at our table. My sister-in-law passed, my brother's wife, and Bess's sister passed back East. And he did not have one kind word to say to either of us. He didn't like Francine. He didn't like Farron. He didn't like them. He thought they were trying to put something over on him. He didn't like me because I didn't bow down. I was too outspoken. He used to look at me. He had Sheila and Jeanette just following him. Maybe it was just that Sheila liked talking to Jeanette and Jeanette liked talking to Willie. They just hung together. I don't know what kind of hold he had on them. Mr. Calhoun made a little comment to Brenda Moran. She came and told me, 'He asked me, "Why do I always talk to them white people?" Why would he ask me something like that?' I said, 'What did you tell him?' She said, 'I didn't pay any attention to him, Marsha.' He said, 'You shouldn't be talking to them. They ain't gonna do nothing for you.' "

Michael Knox says the day it all turned really bad for him and Calhoun was the first visiting day when Calhoun saw his white baby. He said up to that point he got along with him pretty well. They used to talk a little bit even though he knew he was a racist old man. He'd grown up in a bad time in a bad place. He treated him with respect. But, then, that day his wife came with that white baby, that was the end of that.

Calhoun was Calhoun, but he became a concern for me when the jurors were dropping and suddenly it got down to just two. "I was going to have to write a letter," Marsha remembers. "I said, 'Armanda, sweetie, we're getting down to the wire here. Folks are dropping. I tell you, sweetie, I don't know if I'm supposed to or not and I can't ever prove if somebody is as racist as I think they are. But I truly believe in my heart that if they put #165 up there with us, I'm going to have to write a letter and say something.' Because the trial wouldn't be fair. It wouldn't be fair at all.

"When the three deputies were dismissed, I later found out from Jeanette that it was over some racial content," Marsha continues. "People didn't know that we had taken that very hard and that's why the next day some of us wore the black outfits. They were three white deputies and you had mostly black people who were dressed in black. So, if that's racism, then I guess I am a part of racism. We enjoyed those deputies. They never, ever treated any of us different than any of the other jurors. I never saw any type of racism in those deputies. Those were some good people. I was very disappointed. That was one of the first times where I really felt like I just wanted to go home. I felt like these people are wrong. They're wrong for dismissing these deputies. They're wrong for taking our deputies from us. I didn't know why they were dismissed at the time. I didn't find that out until later. But I knew something was wrong because right before that, they dismissed Jeanette. I knew she was trying to stir up some stuff about not being able to go to the gym. It was all just lies. It was all wrong. I was there. There was no hatred in that man's heart. Deputy McDonald, Deputy Mathews, or Deputy Tokar. They were all very good people. I hope that they were able to get positions that they liked. I hope that this didn't tarnish their records because they were some very good people and I stand behind them still.

"I wrote a letter to Judge Ito about the concerns I had about the dismissal of the three deputies. I sort of felt like it was due to some type of goings-on that Jeanette was stirring up. I couldn't quite put my finger on it. I knew that she didn't like them. Then they were dismissed. So, you put two and two together. She was a hell-raiser. She could raise some hell."

While Jeanette and Willie did feel the deputies exhibited racism, others did not. "I didn't experience anything like that," says Michael Knox, who was dismissed March 1. "I give those guys a lot of credit. I enjoyed them and I think that they enjoyed me. I didn't know at the time why I was being observed so closely, but I didn't see any racial prejudice or any special dealings by any one deputy toward one group."

"Without a doubt," Willie Cravin contends. "There was one incident where myself and two black jurors were playing dominos and the deputy who was on in the evening came in. He just passed by the room we were sitting in playing dominos. He left and a few minutes later one of the white deputies came into the room and just sat there and watched us play dominos. I said, 'Why are you just sitting here? You want to play?' He said, 'No.' I said, 'Why are you sitting here?' And he said, 'Well, the other deputy told me to come in here and sit down because nobody's supposed to be in the room by themselves.' So I said, 'Oh, okay.' Then the next night, when I'm watching a movie across the hall, there were five non-black jurors in the same room and they were all in a huddle. But there was no deputy sitting with them. The same deputy who came in the night before and sent the other deputy to sit with us, he passed through and saw all of the non-black jurors sitting in the room, but he didn't send a deputy in there. There were other incidents, too."

After the deputies left, Judge Ito interviewed us. Matter of fact, we told the sergeant that we were not going to work until we talked to him. He called us in one by one. When he called us in, everybody voiced their opinion on how these deputies were dismissed and that at no time had they exhibited any type of racism toward us. We thought that it was unfair that he did what he did.

As far as racism goes, I think there has been a visible change, but I think there are still some hidden agendas out there. I think there are a lot of people out there who weren't a part of the sixties, but they are really struggling, trying to make a difference. I think there are enough of them out there that we can all make a difference. But racism is still there. Somehow you think it will always be there, but consciously you hope that it won't be. The fact that years ago people wouldn't even talk about it, but now they are talking about it, which is an improvement in itself. Maybe, just maybe the fact that we are talking about it and making a lot more people aware that it still exists, maybe we can make changes. Maybe that's something positive that this trial has helped bring out.

I think that's what it is going to take, because racism starts in the cradle when you start feeding this stuff to your children. If we can start talking about it, we can start feeding our children positiveness. That a human being is a human being no matter what color they are. Then maybe generations down the line we can get a lot better, break this barrier we've had all these hundreds of years. I hope so because a lot of times in life you have to lose things in order to gain things. As I said earlier, though, I do feel badly, very badly for the families and that weighs on my mind. But if out of all of this we can get some kind of unity in our country within our families, within ourselves even, then we can get our country unified. And I think if we can do that, we have done a hell of a thing.

12

A POST-VERDICT FORUM

In the weeks following the end of the O.J. Simpson murder trail, jurors Armanda Cooley, Carrie Bess, Marsha Rubin-Jackson, Jeanette Harris, Willie Cravin, Michael Knox, Tracy Kennedy, and Tracy Hampton answered key questions posed by regular citizens, a panel of legal experts, and social commentators who had followed the case throughout its entirety. Each member of the forum—renowned trial attorney Melvin Belli; jury expert and author of What Makes Juries Listen, *Sonya Hamlin; noted civil rights attorney Leo Terrell; Loyola University law professor Stanley Goldman; Court TV anchor Rikki Klieman; attorney and legal consultant for Fox Television Jay Monahan; talk show host, and social commentator Geraldo Rivera; divorce attorney Raoul Felder, and others—had the opportunity to ask one question. Both jurors and dismissed jurors responded with their opinions.*

MARVIN BELLI, attorney:

> *Do you believe that O.J. Simpson is guilty but that you chose to vote not guilty because the case wasn't proven beyond a reasonable doubt?*

"Based on the information that was presented, I felt that there was a lot of evidence that pointed to Mr. Simpson's guilt—for example, the blood, there was no question in my mind that it was

193

Mr. Simpson's," says Armanda. "There were so many questions in my mind, however, and because we had no direct evidence and had to go on circumstantial evidence, I had no alternative at that time but to think he was not guilty. And it is important to remember that a not guilty verdict requires just one thing that can create reasonable doubt. We had much more than that. There were many questions that were not answered."

"I don't believe Mr. Simpson did it," Marsha states flatly. "But I do think he knew or knows something about it. So, no, I don't think he is guilty of the actual crime, but I think he is guilty in the sense that he does know something about it."

Carrie adds, "I feel that if Mr. Simpson did it, he had an assistant. I'm not saying I believe he committed the murders; I'm just saying that I don't believe he did it by himself if he was there. I believe there was more than one person there, and if it was O.J. Simpson, he did have some assistance in getting rid of the evidence."

"You know I've never come to terms one way or the other," says Jeanette Harris. "I didn't know O.J. Simpson before the trial. It's not like I can say, 'He's not capable of such an act.' It's not like I can say, 'Yeah, that sounds like something he'd do.' I wasn't there. I have never come to a position where I would say: 'He did it,' or 'He didn't do it.' I doubt that I will ever get to that position. I didn't know him personally."

"I think someone else committed those two murders," says Willie Cravin. "It's hard for me to fathom that one individual would go there and kill one person—cut their throat and then stab Ron Goldman thirty-one times. To me if one person is killing somebody and I come up the sidewalk and I see this I'm leaving. There is no way I'm going to come up here and let that person kill me too. Or if I see something happening, I'm going to go and get some help. There was a maid next door. I think there was more than one murderer who caused these people to die."

"I personally think he did it," says Tracy Kennedy. "I'm not sure if it was proven beyond a reasonable doubt but that's just my personal gut feeling in my heart."

Michael Knox isn't as clear. "To the extent of him actually committing the crime I think that the defense did an excellent job of arguing reasonable doubt and I think that was what acquitted O.J., but the forensic and all the other evidence put him at the crime scene," he says. "That was indisputable. Without a doubt he was definitely there. The shoe print; the gloves I do believe were definitely his. The fiber in the Bronco and all the other evidence definitely put him at the crime scene. Whether he actually committed that crime without having a weapon as evidence is hard to prove and I think that's what the defense played off of was the reasonable doubt theory, and when they got into the DNA evidence unfortunately the mishandling of a lot of the evidence by L.A.P.D. really took their case southward."

SONYA HAMLIN, jury expert and author of *What Makes Juries Listen*:

> *Did you change your mind about Simpson's guilt or innocence at any point in the case, and if so, when?*

"Actually, I felt that Mr. Simpson was guilty when the prosecutors were putting on their case. But when direct examination came about and poked holes in the evidence, that brought a lot of questionable things to my mind," Armanda replies. "I turned to the fact that, well, maybe he is not guilty. One of the crucial moments where I changed my thinking was when I heard evidence about the glove. The testimony about the drying time of blood on leather was that it would take anywhere from three to four hours, and the glove was not picked up until seven or seven and a half hours later. Another issue was about the blood drops on the socks and the location of the drops. Another episode that changed my mind was basically the picking up of the evidence weeks later and when they tested it, the results were so much different—the DNA content being so much different than the original drops were."

"I had never really formed an opinion during the case," Marsha insists. "After we had heard about the DNA and all the blood evidence, the part about Mr. Simpson's cut finger and the glove not being cut, and during Mr. Parks' testimony were times when I could have gone either way," Marsha says. "You see, I had a lot of questions in my mind when I went to deliberate. So it was not until I got in that deliberation room that I actually formed my opinion."

Carrie says: "I had ups and downs quite a few times because, when they first started on the case, they had O.J.'s cut finger on the left side, with the Bruno Magli shoe, with the blood drops falling right next to it, and I believed that Mr. Simpson was guilty. But then here comes the defense saying the blood was degraded, they never found any Bruno Magli shoes, and there was EDTA in some of the drops. That posed a problem for me. Second, I could not figure out who could leave a scene that was so bloody, get rid of clothes, leave some evidence, and never track anything—not even a blade of grass—in the house. Even though he left blood in the Bronco, I couldn't see how you could manage not to leave some blood somewhere, up the stairs or somewhere as you changed clothes. Even on the tiles in the bathroom. I could never understand that."

LEO TERRELL, civil rights attorney:

Now that you've been dismissed, have you heard anything that was not admitted that either confirmed your belief in O.J.'s innocence or changed your mind?

"Like everyone else, I've heard a lot of things that we didn't get to hear during sequestration. But nothing that I've heard changed my mind," says Armanda. "What I hate is that a lot of that information I did not receive I think would have been important information to me. I'm not saying that the same reasonable doubt issues may not have come up, but I think I would have weighed them a little bit differently. Who knows? You don't know how it would have been presented by the prosecution or defense, so based on that, I can't say my response would be any different."

Marsha adds: "I have heard since I've been out about the money, the wig, the beard and the travel kit, the visa, the passport, and then him going to the grave [on the day of the chase] . . . that makes me believe that he truly did know something about the murders. I still don't think that he did it, but he knows something a whole lot more about it, though. If a lot of the evidence had been brought out, for instance, the diaries that contained examples of abuse and the evidence in the Bronco, I would have given that a lot more thought."

Jeanette Harris agrees. "The ten thousand dollars, the passport, the fake beard, the fibers from the Bronco, Nicole's word from her diary, all those things I believe should have been presented to the jury," she says. "I have a problem with the judicial system presenting itself—presenting the truth, the whole truth, and nothing but the truth. The whole truth was not an issue. And to put those people in that position to say make a decision based on the evidence and only giving them a part of the evidence was very unfair to the jury."

"I am still to this day in awe as to why some information did not come in as evidence," says Michael Knox. "I can't understand that, and I think all of that definitely would have made a difference in the verdict. I think that is something that all of America has asked themselves and will continue: If you are innocent of a crime and you were just visiting a grave site, then why the fake beard, why all the cash, why the gun, why all of that?"

"Anything relating to the case should have been made available to the jurors," argues Tracy Hampton. "Later on I found out that there was five or ten thousand dollars for O.J., and the fake beard, and his Bronco, and also the Fuhrman tapes, all of that should have been played to the jurors. Anything relating to the case that was important, and I felt that those things were important and should have been made available to the jurors."

"Since I've been out, I'm dealing with a lot more things that I had no idea were involved," says Carrie. "Some of them, it was like they broke us off a piece of it and brought it into the court and we were left to decipher between what was positive and what was negative. I was shocked, truly shocked, over a lot of the evidence that was held from us, because I would have thought if they were truly trying to get to the root of this case, they would have brought everything to us. But, you know, from what we got and from what I learned, it was broken. It's been picked. I don't know how the defense would have handled it but I would have given it a lot more consideration because what we had to deal with was no comparison to what they had on the outside."

Armanda adds: "One more comment on that. The prosecution was trying to build up a case based on the rage that Mr. Simpson had built up through the time periods between 1985 and 1994, and the information they gave us about that period of spousal abuse was really just not enough information to indicate that this man had built up all this rage over all this time. We only had one incident with three little episodes, and it wasn't until we got out that we heard about all these other incidents. I hear about these other episodes and I'm thinking, *Well, damn, I can truly see spousal abuse or some type of rage will build up within a person if I would have heard all this stuff.* And if we knew about the drug buy and all that, well, you could put all that in its proper perspective and you can see where somebody . . . that he may have been in a rage and pissed off enough to do those types of things."

STAN GOLDMAN, professor of law at Loyola University:

Did you have your mind made up before the trial?

Carrie: "Oh, we can answer that as one: Heavens, no."

GOLDMAN:

Well, then, would it have made any difference had the defense not called any witnesses?

"Aloha," Marsha adds. "Had the defense not called any witnesses, I believe that the prosecution would have had a grand case."

"It would have made a lot of difference," says Carrie. "We'd have said bon voyage to O.J."

RIKKI KLIEMAN, attorney and Court TV anchor:

Did any of you ever learn that Mark Fuhrman took the fifth amendment before you reached a verdict? What did you think when Fuhrman was not recalled to the witness stand?

"No, I never heard that," says Armanda. "At first I didn't really think anything, because there were still certain other witnesses who I was waiting to hear from, like Faye Resnick, Al Cowlings— you know, people they had mentioned in the beginning in the opening statements. But my first impression about Mr. Fuhrman was that he was lying from the beginning and I just didn't have any faith in his testimony from jump street, so I didn't think it was necessary for me to even hear from him again. When he walked on the stand immediately I knew that the man was a snake. It's just something that hit me. I'm saying, 'Don't prejudge the man, Armanda. Give him an opportunity. But they tell you over and over again, as jurors, do not leave your common sense out the door. Use your gut feeling.' "

"It didn't matter," Marsha says. "In fact, I really didn't think anything of it at all when Fuhrman was not recalled. Because once they had brought the tapes out, there was no need for him to even come back up there—we knew the man had lied."

"Up until they brought the tapes out, I thought O.J. was gone," says Carrie. "Because I really had not discredited Fuhrman, I really hadn't. I just figured here's a sharp cop. This guy was really on it and he was just lucky enough to find every damn thing when it came to the evidence. I'm just figuring that he's one of those lucky cops . . . that he must have been a hell of a detective, and then I come to find out he was a, you know . . ."

Marsha adds, "His getting up there saying he had never said nigger and I'm thinking, *Oh, come on now, I know you're lying about that.* It didn't discredit his whole testimony to me. But after they had validated the tapes and the court had confirmed they were his tapes, there was no need for them to bring him back."

JAY MONAHAN, attorney and legal consultant for Fox Television:

What did you think when Detective Vannatter testified that Mark Fuhrman told him that Kato had talked about thumps on the wall, after hearing Fuhrman testify he never told Vannatter that Kato had told him?

"My feeling was, I sort of felt like I said earlier, that Fuhrman was a liar and I had problems with him," explains Armanda. "Because as long as he was being interviewed by the prosecution, as I indicated before, he was cool and suave as could be. I mean, he looked good up there. And I knew the man was a professional witness and all of that, that he had been trained to testify. I couldn't really figure out why they had trained him until he was cross-examined. Then I could see that the man's breathing patterns had changed because his tie was just jumping. And I figured, why is he so excited now, what happened to his cool and calmness? So, I had sort of discredited him in my mind. The judge tells you not to form any opinion about the case, you don't really form an opinion, but what you are doing is analyzing each witness who comes up to that stand and trying to determine is this person telling the truth or are they just sitting up here trying to, you know, b.s. somebody. So I had sort of discredited him and probably Vannatter from the beginning."

Carrie responds: "Number one, that was confusing testimony that was torn apart by both the prosecutors and the defense. Vannatter stating that Fuhrman told him what he was doing, that when he was talking with Kato, Fuhrman came around and told him that he was gonna go and check out things. Then he comes back and says that Vannatter didn't know anything about what he was doing. Vannatter has been found to prevaricate in two incidents in this case, so I'm really not surprised to find that. You have to really discredit these two police officers."

"Well, on that note, I don't really recall the order in which way they went, but I know that one of them had said that they were wrong, that they didn't concur on how the events had happened," Marsha says. "But what brought my attention to those two was when they said they had come through that back door off the pool into the house. Then Arnelle Simpson got on the stand and said that she had to go around to undo the alarm system and they entered through the front door. They both had said they had come through the back gate, off the pool doors. So their whole testimony didn't really hold any weight with me after I got into the deliberation room. I figured those two were trying to cover for each other. I don't know if they were in any type of conspiracy, you know, but conspiring to cover for each other, yes."

GERALDO RIVERA, talk-show host:

How can you explain away O.J.'s blood at the murder scene, found hours before his blood sample was taken?

"We can't explain it away. I don't think anybody has really tried to explain it away. Me, personally, I have not tried to explain it away at all. That was not one of the issues and that was definitely not the reasonable doubt we based our decision on," says Armanda.

"Okay, now that's exactly what I meant by me believing. I had no doubt in my mind that that wasn't O.J.'s blood, the blood drops," says Marsha. "But by them being so degraded they could have been there before. Prior to the murders. He visited that place often. See, the first blood they found was the blood that was on the gate, two, three days later, or two weeks later. Samples 47, 48, 49, 50, 52 were all degraded. It could have been there prior to the murders."

Carrie says, "Well, like I stated, the blood by the shoe print are the drops that they talked about. I didn't have a problem with it being the same type as O.J.'s, but the only thing I had a problem with was that it was so degraded you couldn't read some of it. Most of it you couldn't read. The part that they really read, which I think were samples 50 and 52 coming out the back gate, was the only drops that they really, really could say was O.J.'s and the one that was on the fence that had EDTA in it. And I really can't speak out for that because they never tested to see what the kids' blood drops were. They never compared anybody else's blood."

Armanda interrupts: "Excuse me. But there was testimony from the fingerprint man, there were a lot of fingerprints there that they never did find out who they belonged to."

"There was so much degradation in that blood that they could never really pinpoint it to say this is the type it was," says Carrie. "And when they got to the autorads, to say these are his drops, they still had a problem, saying that some of it was so weak that they couldn't even say so. On that point, I can't say one way or the other. I feel like maybe if they had gone to Rockingham instead of Bundy, we all might know whether or not it was really O.J.'s blood."

RAOUL FELDER:

Which lawyer did you dislike most, and how did this affect your decision?

"I don't think we disliked anyone," Marsha says. "But I do think some of us were offended when the District Attorney's office sent Chris Darden down. I remember feeling that I thought he was sent down to be part of the prosecution as a token because the jury was predominantly black. He wasn't there right at the start— through selection and all—and I thought the prosecution felt they needed this particular balance."

"I didn't dislike any of them. I didn't dislike them personally, but I disliked Marcia Clark's mannerisms at times," says Marsha. "She showed me that the defense was frustrating her, that they were wearing her down, which is too bad because I think she is a grand lawyer. She presented a great case. But I could just see frustration with her. I could see the sighs she would give when they would just wear her down. But I didn't dislike her and it had no effect on my decision at all. I didn't dislike any lawyer. Right now, if I had a problem I would hire any one of them. I thought they all did an outstanding job."

"Well, I have no reason to dislike any of them. But I didn't particularly care for Chris Darden's mannerisms toward the jurors and how he treated some of us," says Carrie. "Really. I thought Chris at times was very sarcastic. I thought he was . . . you know, with some of the witnesses I didn't think he was so nice. I didn't think it was professional at times."

ROBERT KENT, writer and high school teacher in South Central Los Angeles:

Do you believe that the removal of any juror or jurors was due to jury tampering by either the defense or the prosecution?

"Without a doubt," says Jeanette Harris. "After we were first selected, I saw a tape of Gil Garcetti. He was asked, 'How do you feel about having a predominately African-American jury?' And he said, 'That jury is not going to render the verdict.' To me he had plans somewhere. I believe that from day one they knew that I wasn't gonna be there at the end of the case. They knew that Willie Cravin wasn't gonna be there at the end of the case. They knew that Michael Knox wasn't gonna be there at the end of the case. I think that there was this plan and I can't for the life of me understand why they even put us there in the first place if they knew that they were not gonna use us until the end.

"I guess it's possible that they may have had an equal agenda," continues Harris. "When I was dismissed I knew that somebody targeted me but I didn't know if it was the defense or the prosecution, so I suppose the defense may have had some jurors that they figured were not good for their cause and had them dismissed. It's possible."

"In my situation, yes, I know I was," says Willie Cravin. "I don't know about the others. I heard some of the others had stated that they were writing books or some had written notes and these were things that the judge had admonished them not to do. Now, Tracy Hampton she asked to be removed. In my case I felt that I hadn't done anything so I didn't feel that I should be removed but the others I don't know. Jeanette had said that she felt that it was something that didn't concern domestic violence. She felt that she was dismissed unjustly because the court perceived one thing and she perceived another."

"I personally believe that once the trial gets started," says Tracy Kennedy, "you leave the jurors alone and let them do what they are supposed to do without having to worry about their past and what insignificant thing they may have said or have done. I don't know but I think some of the alternate jurors were finagling ways of getting jurors dismissed so that they could get on the regular jury. I think—I don't remember her name now, Catherine Murdoch, was unjustly dismissed. I think that I was unjustly dismissed. I think that Willie Cravin was unjustly dismissed and possibly one or two more. I'm not sure but I suspect that it was because of alternate jurors finagling."

"Manipulating the jury was obvious from the outset," remembers Michael Knox. "Well, I saw the prosecution and the defense trying to orchestrate the jury to their liking and that's only natural. But I think that after the jury was selected the prosecution personally had a problem with the make-up. And I know I started receiving stares and glares that I didn't understand at the time from Marcia Clark."

GLENN PETERSON, media critic and social commentator:

Do you believe Judge Ito exhibited a lack of control over the trial?

"I think if he had showed more control from the beginning, the trial would have been over sooner but as the trial started out it seemed to be the judge and everyone was playing to the press," says Willie Cravin. "They were playing to the media. They were playing to the public and it caused a lot of delays as far as the trial was concerned. I can recall beepers, cellular phones going off in the audience. People were laughing. It was like a show for a while there. The judge would make comments and the audience would laugh. Some of the attorneys would make comments and the audience would laugh. And a murder trial, I'm thinking, you gonna get down to business so that we can get on because once you bring the laugh element in and you start to lose control, then once you lose control then things just start to escalate, you know, first one thing, then another."

Jeanette Harris agrees. "I think that it is wonderful to be a nice person and to give all this leeway to people but Judge Ito—that's not something that should be in the courtroom," she remarks. "I think that judges should have total control; time should be an issue. He would allow people and attorneys and whatever to go on and on and on and on, and then he would come to you and apologize and after a while those apologies were, you know, you had a deaf ear. 'Oh, I'm sorry that we have gone on with this such a long time.' And you would go out, 'Oh, I'm sorry.' And you would go out and then, 'Oh, I'm sorry.' So you would want to stand up and say, 'Well, why don't you just do something as opposed to being sorry.' So, yeah, he should have had much more control over the trial."

"I don't want to play Monday morning quarterback about Judge Ito because I have the highest respect for him but I think he lost control in the courtroom and I don't think he ever regained it," says Tracy Kennedy. "I'm not of a legal mind but I saw him make two or three controversial or contradictory decisions in a matter of a couple of hours and that made me pause and question the legal ramifications of that. I think every time Mr. Simpson got up to give a demonstration it was out of control. I think whether Judge Ito lost control or not, after Mr. Fung was on the stand it went downhill for the prosecution from then on. I think that most of the sidebars and things like that should have been handled before court or after court. That shouldn't be done while the jury's sitting there watching what is going on because you can see. You can't necessarily hear what's going on over there. I tried to ignore it but you can see body language and things like that that are going on and that has a bearing on the way people think."

"I think that he was maybe too giving to both sides," says Michael Knox, "and there was a point of time where he did lose control and then he tried to gain that control back again and that back and forth, trying to appease both the defense and prosecution and lead to the trial to being as long as it was and also lead to a lot of other things that the public didn't perceive as good jurisprudence."

Tom Greenburg, attorney, Gibson, Dunn, and Crutcher:

Do you believe that Kato Kaelin has knowledge that could lead to the conviction of the person or persons who committed the murders of Nicole Brown Simpson and Ronald Goldman?

"I think that Kato knows a whole lot more than he has spoken of to this date and because he is a friend of O.J.'s and because he was living there rent free, I think that his allegiance to O.J. was apparent," says Michael Knox. "I don't know if Kato knows all the details but I believe he knows more than he has indicated about these murders because as I have stated before I believe that it was done professionally. I believe that O.J. has knowledge of it. And I think where the prosecution made their big mistake was that they accused O.J. solely by himself of committing these murders, and I think there was a rush to judgment as far as the prosecution is concerned. I think if they had taken a little bit more time before they had made an arrest and developed their case a little bit better, they would have come out differently."

"I don't know if Kato Kaelin had knowledge of the actual murderers," says Jeanette Harris, "or if he felt that O.J. was guilty or innocent. Kato Kaelin was somebody who came across as really struggling. I don't know if it's that he was covering up something or if he was in a difficult situation. I personally liked Kato Kaelin but felt that he was between a rock and a hard place. I really sympathized with him. As far as him knowing exactly who committed the murders, I believe that he probably knows something. Exactly what he knows I couldn't say. But I think he knows something and I guess because of his nature, he seems like—I don't want to say a joke—but he's somebody you really feel sorry for—I really felt sorry for him."

"I think that he knows a lot more than what he said on the stand," says Willie Cravin. "He seemed to be unusually nervous. It may be that he was fearful for his life. It may have something to do with his life or something to do with his future which may have prevented him from telling the whole truth. I think he may have told part of the truth but it was like half-truths and not everything."

"I would hate to think that he would have some knowledge that he didn't come forth with," comments Tracy Kennedy. "She (Nicole) was his friend, I understand, and he did seem really reluctant to answer anything while on the stand. I think he was torn between the friendship of Nicole and the friendship of Mr. Simpson. I think he didn't want to be swayed one way or the other. He realized that this was very serious and he didn't want to influence the jury one way or the other, I don't think. I think in that respect he held back."

"I have no idea," Tracy Hampton says. "I don't know; I can't say that I think he has knowledge. I can't say that. But I think when he was on the witness stand he did appear to be a bit uncomfortable; maybe there were things that were left out. I don't know."

JENNY BURMAN, writer and editor:

Were you shocked by the revelations in Nicole's diaries documenting brutal abuse since 1978?

"Everybody had a certain perception of O.J., at least I did prior to the trial," remarks Michael Knox. "I knew nothing about his personal life and I was surprised to know that he had been in a marriage that was abusive—especially when you see people that have the wealth and the prominence that O.J. had prior to this trial you can't imagine them having any problems in life. Sometimes we think that money solves everything but as we have learned in this particular case money doesn't necessarily solve everything.

"No," says Jeanette Harris. "I wasn't shocked with the accusations. I believe that O.J. and Nicole had a very violent relationship and I didn't find that shocking or surprising at all. I kind of felt that that was their relationship before this case."

"O.J. had always been a hero of mine since just before the Rose Bowl game," remembers Tracy Kennedy. "I didn't like it when he ran back that touchdown, I mean that kickoff for a touchdown against Ohio State but outside of that he's always been a hero of mine. I just didn't think his persona as viewed on T.V. and on advertisements doesn't—you just don't perceive him being a person—a violent person or a spouse abuser."

CHRISTINE MAURO, Occupational Therapist:

Do you think it unfair that a woman's own written words, some of it corroborated by independent witnesses, be excluded from the jury as hearsay evidence?

"Well, this is a strange trial," admits Jeanette Harris. "The fact that you were speaking about that being excluded then you look at the other side and everything that Mark Fuhrman said on the tapes was excluded also, so I feel that if they are going to exclude something then, I guess, you can try to be fair to both sides or if you're gonna include everything and then let everything be heard so that both sides are equally represented as far as the trial was concerned."

"Well, I'm not sure that that's not a legal term that I'm not really that certain about," says Tracy Kennedy, "but it seems to me that would be evidence and if it was evidence and corroborated evidence it should have been brought before the jury. But that's my opinion which is a layman's opinion and legal minds—brighter than mine certainly—determined that that was hearsay and not admissible."

"The jury should have heard everything relevant to the case," argues Michael Knox. "I don't know how else to elaborate on that. It seems to me right off the top of my head that it would be relevant. However, the decision was made that it wasn't so I wouldn't—I have the fullest confidence in Judge Ito and I think what was determined relevant was relevant.

"I think that any of the evidence pertaining to this case should have been presented to the jury in order to make a fair and just verdict," remarks Tracy Kennedy. "It was extremely unfair to the jury that things of that nature weren't presented to them. I think that that was important evidence."

"I think not only that evidence but a lot of other evidence that was omitted should have not been omitted," says Tracy Hampton. "I think it would have been better for the jury to have an assessment of the full ramifications of this case if a lot of the evidence had been omitted and it's unfortunate that it wasn't."

CHRIS HEMESATH, writer, editor:

Do you believe the trial went on so long that it affected the verdict?

"Definitely," says Jeanette Harris. "I knew that the deliberations were going to be short but I didn't think that they would be *that* short. I thought maybe two days because what was paramount on the jurors' minds was that 'I want to go home.' Whereas if the trial was shorter, deliberations would have been easier for them and they would have gone on and possibly deliberated where the number one issue is: I want to go home. And we walked in with an April date and here it is October so there is no way that that jury was gonna to deliberate extensively."

"I don't think it affected to the verdict," comments Willie Cravin, "but I think it affected the time of deliberation. I felt the jurors were burnt out. I think they were stressed out. I think they were at their ends. After being sequestered for nine months and being treated worse than prisoners, worse than convicts, I think that the stress factor caught up with them. And I think that once they went to deliberate after being there nine months they took a straw vote and said 'O.K. How many think he's guilty? How many think he's innocent?' And they took a secret ballot and when the jury foreman said that it was ten to two. Then they come back and say 'Well. O.K. Here's the deal. We either go for twelve and '0' or we have a hung jury and we'll be here two more months."

"Absolutely," says Tracy Kennedy. "Had been more than one judge on this or helping with this or directly directing influencing this, I think it would have been much shorter. I personally believe that the cameras in the courtroom were another—that added I would say three months to the trial. I don't think the trial was carried on for the seated jurors and alternates. I think it was carried on for the cameras and the public opinion."

"The length of time that people were cut off from their families—from the world—from the media—from a normal lifestyle affected them," says Michael Knox. "People began to gravitate to whoever was the strongest individual and the weaker individuals on the jury began to take on the persona personalty of the stronger ones and the individuality that I think that we seek as a jury system left a long time ago and people who were weaker gravitated to the stronger ones and the stronger ones influenced that final verdict."

ANGELA FASICK, associate professor at John Carroll University

Do you believe that jurors heard things by way of pillow talk during conjugal visits or through telephone conversations with friends and family?

"When I was a juror," recalls Jeanette Harris, "I personally I didn't engage in pillow talk and from my own point of view the last thing I wanted to talk about when I saw my family was the case. It's something that you're saturated with day by day, all day long and you're missing your family. So, pillow talk about the case was not something that I wanted to engage in. It's not that farfetched however because the possibility was great."

"I know I didn't because I asked my wife not to keep up with the trial," says Tracy Kennedy, "so she wouldn't inadvertently say anything that I shouldn't know or hear. The opportunity certainly was there. I would hope not. I couldn't say if that was done because no one that I knew of said anything that I heard that could have been construed to be talk from the outside. The opportunity was certainly there while speaking on the phone. I thought at the time that everything was closely monitored. We thought our conversations were being taped or videoed in the room during conjugal visits. They wanted us to think that and we thought that.

"You know that would be hard for me to elaborate on," says Michael Knox. "I was released on March 1 and the first conjugal visit that my wife and I had indicated to her that we could not talk about this even in bed because I had taken an oath and to be quite honest with you I thought that our rooms were bugged. There were cameras in the hallways and we did not talk about the trial and as far as the other jurors are concerned I can't speak for them. I was off the trial March 1. The trial was not over until late September early October so that was at least another six months anything could have happened.

"I don't believe that they did," says Willie Cravin, "but then you can't rule out the possibility because they did have visitors and on conjugal visits you were in your room with whoever your visitor was but by the same token I feel that they had listening devices inside of each jurors room and I think the jurors were admonished about speaking about the case and I felt that they were— most of them were probably thinking about the fact that there was a listening device in here so if we say something they are going to find out about it anyway. There was one incident that occurred with me which made me feel that they were listening to your conversation inside and outside as far as the phone conversation was concerned. I was speaking to my daughter one night and we were just talking on the phone and she said well mom is here would you like to speak to her and I said well yes so she puts her mother on the phone. She says, 'Hi. How are you doing?' I said, 'Fine. How are you?' She said, 'I can't hear you.' But the phone clicked as soon as she got on the phone and I said, 'You can't hear me. I'm speaking louder now.' But she said, 'I can't hear you.' And I said, 'I can barely hear you.' And this went on for about a minute. So I said put Shawna back on the phone. She puts my daughter back on the phone. The phone clicks again and I can hear her as plain as day. So it made me believe that they were in earshot of you listening when you were speaking on the phone plus they were on the inside listening to your phone conversations so I find it hard to believe that someone could say something over the phone without the deputies knowing about it because I think that they were listening on both sides of the phone."

Appendix A

JURORS RENDERING THE VERDICT

Armanda Cooley   #230   Seat 1 ORIGINAL

Yolanda Crawford   #1492   Seat 2

Anise Aschenbach   #1290   Seat 3

David Aldana   #19   Seat 4 ORIGINAL

Marsha Rubin-Jackson #984   Seat 5 ORIGINAL

Lionel "Lon" Cryer   #247   Seat 6

Brenda Moran   #795   Seat 7

Sheila Woods   #1233   Seat 8 ORIGINAL

Carrie Bess   #98   Seat 9 ORIGINAL

Gina Rhodes
Rosborough   #2179   Seat 10

Annie Backman   #63   Seat 11 ORIGINAL

Beatrice Wilson   #2457   Seat 12

TOTAL JURY PANEL OF 24 INCLUDING ALTERNATES

<u>Seat 1:</u>

#230   ARMANDA COOLEY   ORIGINAL
51-year-old single African-American woman. Administrative
Assistant III, contracts monitoring for County of Los Angeles.

<u>Seat 2:</u>

#453   TRACY HAMPTON   ORIGINAL
25-year-old single African-American woman.
TWA flight attendant.
Dismissed May 1, 1995 because she told Judge Ito she couldn't
take it anymore. The next day she was rushed to the hospital
for severe depression.

#1427   FARRON CHAVARRIA
29-year-old single Hispanic woman.
Real-estate appraiser for the County of Los Angeles.
Dismissed June 5, 1995 for passing a note to Francine Florio-
Bunten.

#1492   YOLANDA CRAWFORD
25-year-old single black woman.
County hospital worker.

<u>Seat 3:</u>

#602   TRACY KENNEDY   ORIGINAL
White/Native American male.
Amtrak employee.
Dismissed. March 17, 1995.

#1290   ANISE ASCHENBACH
60-year-old white woman. Retired gas company worker.

<u>Seat 4:</u>

#19   DAVID ALDANA   ORIGINAL
32-year-old married Latino man. Pepsi truck driver.

<u>Seat 5:</u>

#984   MARSHA RUBIN-JACKSON   ORIGINAL
38-year-old married African-American woman. Mail carrier for
U.S. Postal Service

Seat 6:

#228   ROLAND COOPER   ORIGINAL
            48-year-old single African-American male. Worked for Hertz.
            Dismissed January 18, 1995.

#247   LIONEL "LON" CRYER
            43-year-old single African-American man. Telephone company
            employee.

Seat 7:

#462   JEANETTE HARRIS   ORIGINAL
            38-year-old married African-American woman. Employment
            interviewer.
            Dismissed April 4, 1995.

#795   BRENDA MORAN
            44-year-old single African-American woman. Repairs comput-
            ers and printers for Superior Court.

Seat 8:

#1233   SHEILA WOODS   ORIGINAL
            38-year-old single African-American woman. Works as an envi-
            ronmental health specialist.

Seat 9:

#98   CARRIE BESS   ORIGINAL
            53-year-old single African-American woman. Clerk for U.S.
            Postal Service.

Seat 10:

#320   NAME NOT AVAILABLE   ORIGINAL
            38-year-old single Hispanic woman. Mail carrier for U.S. Postal
            Service.
            Dismissed January 18, 1995.

#2017   CATHERINE MURDOCH
            63-year-old white married woman.
            Dismissed February 7, 1995.

#1489   WILLIE CRAVIN
         Married African-American man. Manager of a U.S. Postal
         Service station.
         Dismissed June 5, 1995.

#2179   GINA ROSBOROUGH
         28-year-old married African-American woman. Clerk for U.S.
         Postal Service.

Seat 11:

#63   ANNIE BACKMAN   ORIGINAL
         22-year-old single white woman. Handles insurance claims.

Seat 12:

#620   MICHAEL KNOX   ORIGINAL
         46-year-old married African-American man. Federal Express
         delivery.
         Dismissed March 1, 1995.

#353   FRANCINE FLORIO-BUNTEN
         38-year-old married white woman. Telephone company em-
         ployee.
         Dismissed May 26, 1995.

#2457   BEATRICE WILSON
         71-year-old married African-American woman. Retired clean-
         ing officer.

Alternates

#165   WATSON CALHOUN
         72-year-old married African-American man. Security guard.

#1386   REYKO BUTLER
         25-year-old married white woman. Fire Department recep-
         tionist.

Appendix B

JUROR'S PERSONAL CHECK-OFF LIST

PERSONAL HYGIENE ITEMS
    Toothbrush/toothpaste   _____
    Brush/comb   _____
    Nail clippers/file   _____
    Deodorant   _____
    Shampoo   _____
    Blowdryer   _____
    Curling iron/curlers   _____
    Soap   _____

CLOTHING
    Clothing appropriate for court and leisure time. Keep in
    mind that relatives may visit up to two times a week and
    can bring additional clothing or items as needed.   _____

SHOES
    Shoes appropriate for court and light recreation (walking,
    etc.).   _____

MEDICINE
    Aspirin, prescription medicine, chapstick.   _____

EYEGLASSES, SUNGLASSES   _____

CASH
    Not an excessive amount. Relatives will be allowed to bring
    additional amounts if necessary.   _____

FAMILY PHOTOS   _____

LETTER WRITING MATERIAL   _____

WATCH   _____

MAKE-UP   _____

WALKMAN OR SIMILAR LISTENING DEVICE
    Cassette or CD player only.   _____
    Listening tapes or CDs.   _____

BOOKS, PUZZLES, PLAYING CARDS, GAMES   _____

DO NOT BRING
    AM/FM RADIOS
    MAGAZINES OR NEWSPAPERS
    CAMERAS/VIDEO CAMERAS
    EXPENSIVE JEWELRY
    KEYS

NOTE: *ALL ITEMS MUST BE CHECKED BEFORE CHECKING INTO HOTEL. THIS IS TO ENSURE THAT THE COURT IS SEQUESTERING A JURY THAT IS FREE FROM OUTSIDE INFLUENCES.*

Appendix C

RULES FOR JURORS WHILE STAYING AT THE HOTEL

1. Do not tell your relatives where you are staying.
2. Do not discuss anything related to the case with your relatives.
3. You may only discuss the case after you have heard all the evidence and all jurors are present in the jury room during deliberation.
4. No alcoholic beverages are allowed.
5. One juror per room.
6. Jurors are not allowed to go into other jurors' rooms.
7. While at the hotel, if you need to talk to another juror you must stay in the hallway or go into the TV lounge.
8. All jurors will go to breakfast, lunch, and dinner as a group.
9. All jurors will go to the visiting areas as a group.
10. All jurors will go on field trips (the mall, exercise area, etc.) as a group.
11. TV and phone time ends at 11:00 P.M. Sunday through Thursday nights.
12. TV and phone time ends at 12:00 A.M. on Friday and Saturday nights.
13. Each juror will receive a 15 minute time allotment, to make phone calls, per phone time.
14. All jurors will be in their rooms by 11:00 P.M., Sunday through Thursday nights.
15. All jurors will be in their rooms by 12:00 A.M. on Friday and Saturday nights.
16. If you smoke, you are allowed to smoke only in your own room.
17. All key cards for your assigned hotel room will be issued every morning and collected every night before bed time.

Please understand that these rules are formulated to comply with court regulations as they pertain to jury sequestration.

This is needed to preserve the integrity of the jury and maintain a workable environment for all personnel assigned to this case.

Please remember, if you have some form of extreme emergency, feel free to approach any of the deputies with your problem.

Arrangements have been made to try and accommodate any emergency.

Appendix D

SUPERIOR COURT OF THE STATE OF CALIFORNIA IN AND FOR THE COUNTY OF LOS ANGELES

Date: 23 September 1994
Department 103
Hon. Lance A. Ito, Judge
D. Robertson, Deputy Clerk
People v. Orenthal James Simpson
Case #BA097211

COURT ORDER

Each juror and alternate juror selected to serve in this matter is ordered and directed to:

1. Not to read or listen to or watch any accounts or discussions of this case reported by newspapers, television, radio, or any other news media.

2. Not to visit or view the premises or place where the offense or offenses charged were allegedly committed or any premises or place involved in this case unless directed by the court to do so.

3. Not to converse with other jurors or with anyone else upon any subject connected with the trial unless and until permitted to do so by the court.

4. Not to request, accept, agree to accept, or discuss with any person receiving or accepting, any payment or benefit in consideration for supplying any information concerning this trial for a period of 180 days from the return of a verdict or the termination of the case, whichever is earlier.

5. Promptly report to the court any incident within their knowledge involving an attempt by any persons improperly to influence any member of the jury.

Dated: _____   _____

                                                    Hon. Lance A. Ito

I agree to the above order and understand that if I violate the provisions of this order that I can be ordered to pay a sanction to the court of up to $1,500 for each violation pursuant to Code of Civil Procedure Section 177.5, to reimburse or make payment to the County of Los Angeles for costs caused by a violation pursuant to California Rules of Court, Rule 227, or punished by a fine or imprisonment for contempt pursuant to Code of Civil Procedure Section 1218.

Dated: _____ _____
Juror

SUPERIOR COURT OF THE STATE OF CALIFORNIA
IN AND FOR THE COUNTY OF LOS ANGELES

Date: 12 December 1994
Department 103
Hon. Lance A. Ito, Judge
Deirdre Robertson, Deputy Clerk
People v. Orenthal James Simpson
Case # BA097211

COURT ORDER

During the course of this trial, and until further order of the court, the trial jurors and alternates in this case shall NOT read any newspaper article or other written account including magazines or books or watch any television programs dealing with this case, the defendant or his family, the victims or their families, the attorneys or any other matter concerning this case. The court will distribute to the jurors and alternates the local daily newspaper of their choice, edited to remove any coverage of this case.

Jurors and alternates shall *NOT* listen to any radio programming. Each juror and alternate may listen to audio tapes and compact discs, including books on tape that do not concern this case. Jurors and alternates who need current weather and traffic information may get this information by dialing (213) 962-3279.

Jurors and alternates shall *NOT* watch:

1) *ANY* television news program or news break.

2) *ANY* television "tabloid" program such as *Hard Copy, A Current Affair, Inside Edition, American Journal,* or *Premiere Story.*

3) *ANY* television talk show such as *Marilu, Leeza, Jenny Jones, Sally Jessy Raphael, Oprah, Donahue, Good Morning America, Today, CBS This Morning, The Montel Williams Show, The Maury Povich Show, Ricki Lake, Rolonda, Rush Limbaugh* and *Geraldo.*

4) *ANY* television news magazine program such as *60 Minutes, 20/20, Date-line, Eye to Eye, 48 Hours* or *Primetime Live.*

5) *ANY* entertainment news magazine such as *Entertainment Tonight* and *EXTRA.*

6) CNN, CNN Headline News, CNBC, The E! Channel, *Sports Center* on ESPN, *Press Box* on Prime Ticket, *The News* on MTV, any news or talk show on BET and *Dennis Miller Live* on HBO.

7) *The Tonight Show (Jay Leno)* and *The Late Show with David Letterman.*

Jurors and alternates *MAY* watch:

1) Normal television entertainment programming, including sports and home shopping channels, not excluded above, *however, jurors are strongly cautioned to avoid watching advertisements for upcoming news broadcasts known as "teasers."*

2) Cable or satellite television channels: American Movie Classics, Showtime, Cinemax, The Disney Channel, The Movie Channel, The Shopping Channel, The Family Channel, The Cartoon Channel, Turner Classic Movies, MTV, Discovery Channel, Arts and Entertainment (A&E), Bravo, Lifetime, Nashville, Nickelodeon and Home Box Office.

3) Movies and other programming on videotape that do not involve this case, the defendant or his family, the victims or their families, or the attorneys and their families.

Any questions regarding this order shall be directed to the Clerk of the Court, Mrs. Deirdre Robertson at (213) 974–5726.

Appendix E

THE MURDERS

The following is a summary of the wounds to Nicole Brown Simpson and Ronald Goldman. The information is based on the autopsy and preliminary hearing testimony of Dr. Irwin Golden, the deputy medical examiner of Los Angeles County.

NICOLE BROWN SIMPSON
5'5", 129 pounds

CAUSE OF DEATH
Cutting wound of the neck and multiple stab wounds of the neck.

WEAPON
All wounds could have been inflicted on both victims by the same weapon . . . wounds are consistent with a single-edged knife.

OVERVIEW
Neck cut left to right through the spinal bone.
4 wounds to left neck.
3 scalp wounds.

RONALD GOLDMAN
5'9", 171 pounds

CAUSE OF DEATH
Multiple sharp force injuries, either stab wounds or a combination of both.

WEAPON
All wounds could have been inflicted on both victims by the same weapon . . . wounds are consistent with a single-edged knife.

OVERVIEW
6 wounds to the neck and ears—3 on the right side, 3 on the left side.
2 wounds across throat.
5 face wounds and multiple abrasions.
1 scalp wound.
3 chest wounds.
1 thigh wound.
1 abdomen wound.
Many defensive wounds on both hands.

Appendix F

THE EVIDENCE

Evidence mentioned during the prosecution's opening statements as proof O.J. Simpson murdered Nicole Brown Simpson and Ronald Goldman.

- Bloodstains found on a pair of socks in O.J. Simpson's bedroom—one spot of blood matches O.J. Simpson's blood, another spot matches Nicole Simpson's.

- A total of seven bloodstains found in the Bronco—four were O.J. Simpson's blood, one matched Nicole Simpson's and two were a mixture of O.J. Simpson, Nicole Simpson, and Goldman.

- The glove found on the grounds of O.J. Simpson's estate contained a mixture of blood consistent with the mixture of blood of O.J. Simpson, Nicole Simpson, and Ronald Goldman. The glove also contained hair matching Nicole Simpson and Goldman, and fibers similar to those found in Bronco carpet and on Goldman's shirt.

- Blood drops at the crime scene leading away from the bodies—five drops match O.J. Simpson's blood.

- The ski cap found at the crime scene contained fibers like those from the carpet of the Bronco and hairs like those of O.J. Simpson.

- Ronald Goldman's shirt contained hairs like those of O.J. Simpson.

- Two bloodstains found in O.J. Simpson's driveway matched his blood.

- Bloodstains found in O.J. Simpson's house matched his blood.

Appendix G

PROSECUTION WITNESSES

Prosecution witnesses in the O.J. Simpson murder trial and the dates of their testimony.

Sharyn Gilbert, L.A.P.D. 911 Dispatcher	January 31, 1995
Det. John Edwards, L.A.P.D.	January 31, 1995
Det. Mike Farrell, L.A.P.D.	January 31, 1995
Ronald Shipp, friend of O.J. Simpson and Nicole Simpson	February 1 and 2, 1995
Terri Moore, 911 operator	February 2, 1995
Sgt. Robert Lerner, L.A.P.D.	February 3, 1995
Catherine Boe, neighbor of Nicole Brown Simpson	February 3, 1995
Carl Colby, neighbor of Nicole Brown Simpson	February 3, 1995
Denise Brown, sister of Nicole Brown Simpson	February 3 and 6, 1995
Candace Garvey, friend of Nicole Brown Simpson	February 6, 1995
Cynthia Shahian, friend of Nicole Brown Simpson	February 6, 1995
Tia Gavin, waitress at Mezzaluna restaurant	February 7, 1995
Stuart Tanner, bartender at Mezzaluna restaurant	February 7, 1995
Karen Crawford, manager at Mezzaluna restaurant	February 7, 1995
Pablo Fenjves, neighbor of Nicole Brown Simpson	February 7, 1995
Eva Stein, neighbor of Nicole Brown Simpson	February 8, 1995
Louis Karpf, neighbor of Nicole Brown Simpson	February 8, 1995
Steven Schwab, neighbor of Nicole Brown Simpson	February 8, 1995
Sukru Boztepe, neighbor of Nicole Brown Simpson	February 8, 1995
Elsie Tistaert, neighbor of Nicole Brown Simpson	February 8, 1995
Mark Storfer, neighbor of Nicole Brown Simpson	March 6, 1995 (called out of order)

Officer Robert Riske, L.A.P.D.	February 9 and 14, 1995
Sgt. David Rossi, L.A.P.D.	February 14 and 15, 1995
Det. Ronald Phillips, L.A.P.D.	February 15–17, 1995
Det. Tom Lange, L.A.P.D.	February 17, 1995 February 21–23, 1995 March 6–9, 1995
Detective Mark Fuhrman, L.A.P.D.	March 9 and 10, 1995 March 13–16, 1995
Lt. Frank Spangler, L.A.P.D.	March 16, 1995
Detective Philip Vannatter, L.A.P.D.	March 16 and 17, 1995 March 20 and 21, 1995
Patti Goldman (Ron Goldman's stepmother)	March 9, 1995
Darryl Smith, freelance cameraman working for "Inside Edition"	March 16, 1995
Brian "Kato" Kaelin, O.J. Simpson houseguest	March 21–23, 1995 March 27 and 28, 1995
Rachel Ferrara, friend of Brian Kaelin	March 28, 1995
Allan Parks, limousine driver	March 28 and 29, 1995
Judge Delbert Wong, Special Master	March 29, 1995
James Williams, skycap at L.A. International Airport	March 29, 1995
Susan Silva, Westec Security	March 30, 1995
Charles Cale, neighbor of O.J. Simpson	March 31, 1995
Dennis Fung, L.A.P.D. criminalist	April 3–5, 1995 April 11–14, 1995 April 17–18, 1995
Andrea Mazzola, L.A.P.D. criminalist	April 20, 1995 April 25–27, 1995
Gregory Matheson, chief forensic chemist, L.A.P.D.	May 1–5, 1995
Bernie Douroux, towtruck driver	May 8, 1995
Robin Cotton, laboratory director of Cellmark Diagnostics	May 8–15, 1995
Gary Sims, California Department of Justice	May 16–22, 1995 May 31–June 1, 1995

Renee Montgomery, criminalist, CA Dept. of Justice   May 23 and 24, 1995

Collin Yamauchi, criminalist, L.A.P.D.   May 24–31, 1995

Dr. Lakshamanan Sathyavagiswaran, Los Angeles
County Chief Medical Examiner   June 2–15, 1995

Brenda Vemich, buyer, Bloomingdale's   June 15, 1995

Richard Rubin, former vice president, Aris Isotoner   June 15 and 16, 1995

William Bodziak, nationally recognized shoe print expert   June 19, 1995

Samuel Poser, shoe dept. manager, Bloomingdale's   June 20, 1995

LuEllen Robertson, fraud control & security,
Airtouch Cellular Phones   June 21, 1995

Kathleen Delaney, Mirage Hotel   June 21, 1995

Bruce Weir, population geneticist   June 22 and 23, 1995
June 26, 1995

Denise Lewis, criminalist, L.A.P.D.   June 26 and 27, 1995

Susan Brockbank, criminalist, L.A.P.D.   June 27 and 28, 1995

Douglas Deedrick, FBI Analyst   June 29–July 6, 1995

REBUTTAL WITNESSES:

Mark Krueger, photographed Simpson in 1990   September 11, 1995

Bill Renken, professional photographer   September 11, 1995

Kevin Schott, photography teacher   September 11, 1995

Stewart West, former professional photographer   September 11, 1995

Debra Guidera, photographed Simpson in Dec., 1993   September 11, 1995

Michael Romano, professional photographer   September 11, 1995

Richard Rubin, former vice president, Aris Isotoner   September 12, 1995

Gary Sims, senior criminologist, CA Dept. of Justice   September 13, 1995

Theresa Ramirez, photographed interview with
Thano Peratis   September 13, 1995

Douglas Deedrick, FBI Analyst   September 14, 1995

William Bodziak, FBI Special Agent   September 14 and 15, 1995
September 18, 1995

Keith Bushey, commander, L.A.P.D.   September 20, 1995

Appendix H

DEFENSE WITNESSES

The defense witnesses in the O.J. Simpson murder trial and the dates of their testimony.

Arnelle Simpson, O.J. Simpson's daughter from his first marriage	July 10, 1995
Carmelita Simpson-Durio, O.J. Simpson's sister	July 10, 1995
Eunice Simpson, O.J. Simpson's mother	July 10, 1995
Carol Conner, philanthropist and songwriter	July 10, 1995
Mary Collins, O.J. Simpson's longtime interior designer	July 10, 1995
Shirley Simpson-Baker, O.J. Simpson's older sister	July 11, 1995
Jack McKay, a psychological association executive, played golf with O.J. Simpson on June 8, 1994	July 11, 1995
Dan Mandel, walked with his date, Ellen Aaronson, near Nicole Brown Simpson's home about 10:25 P.M. on the night of the murders	July 11, 1995
Ellen Aaronson, walked with date, Danny Mandel, near Nicole Brown Simpson's home about 10:25 P.M. on the night of the murders	July 11, 1995
Denise Pilnak, lived on 900 block of Bundy near Nicole Brown Simpson's condominium	July 11, 1995
Judy Telander, friend of Denise Pilnak and was with her on the night of the murders	July 11, 1995
Robert Heidstra, neighbor of Nicole Brown Simpson	July 11 and 12, 1995
Wayne Stanfield, American Airlines Captain	July 12, 1995
Michael Norris, Los Angeles Airport delivery service employee	July 12, 1995
Michael Gladden, Los Angeles Airport delivery service employee	July 12, 1995
Howard Bingham, passenger on flight from Los Angeles to Chicago	July 13, 1995

Stephen Valerie, passenger on flight from Los Angeles to Chicago	July 13, 1995
Jim Merrill, Hertz employee who picked up Simpson at Chicago's O'Hare airport	July 13, 1995
Dave Kilduff, Hertz employee who saw Simpson outside his hotel in Chicago	July 13, 1995
Mark Partridge, passenger on flight from Chicago to Los Angeles	July 13, 1995
Dr. Robert Huizenga, Beverly Hills private physician	July 14, 1995 July 17 and 18, 1995
Juanita Moore, O.J. Simpson's hairdresser	July 18, 1995
Officer Donald Thompson, L.A.P.D.	July 18, 1995
John Meraz, towed Ford Bronco	January 19, 1995 July 19, 1995
Richard Walsh, fitness trainer in exercise video	July 19, 1995
Willie Ford, L.A.P.D. videographer	July 19 and 20, 1995
Josephine "Gigi" Guarin, O.J. Simpson's housekeeper	July 20, 1995
Det. Kelly Mulldorfer, L.A.P.D.	July 20, 1995
Det. Adalberto Luper, L.A.P.D.	July 20, 1995
Dr. Fredric Rieders, forensic toxicologist	July 24, 1995 August 14, 1995
Roger Martz, FBI Special Agent	July 25 and 26, 1995
Herbert MacDonell, blood splatter expert	July 27, 1995 July 31 and August 1, 1995
Thano Peratis, jail nurse (taped testimony)	August 1, 1995
John Gerdes, clinical director, Immunological Associates, Denver	August 2–4, 1995 August 7, 1995
Terence Speed, defense statistics professor	August 7 and 8, 1995
Dr. Michael Baden, forensic pathologist	August 10 and 11, 1995
Michele Kestler, director, L.A.P.D. crime lab	August 14 and 16, 1995
Gilbert Aguilar, L.A.P.D. fingerprint specialist	August 17, 1995

John Larry Ragle, former director, Orange County
Sheriff's Department Crime Laboratory   August 21, 1995

Christian Reichardt, friend of O.J. Simpson and former
boyfriend of Faye Resnick   August 22, 1995

Detective Kenneth Berris, Chicago Police Department August 22, 1995

Dr. Henry Lee, chief criminalist, state of
Connecticut   August 22 and 23, 1995
                                         August 25 and 28, 1995

Kathleen Bell, heard Mark Fuhrman utter racial slurs   September 5, 1995

Natalie Singer, heard Mark Fuhrman utter racial slurs September 5, 1995

William Blasini, Jr., general manager,
wholesale parts shop   September 5, 1995

Laura Hart McKinney, professor and
screenwriter   September 5 and 6, 1995

Roderic Hodge, individual arrested by Mark Fuhrman   September 6, 1995

Det. Philip Vannatter, L.A.P.D.   September 20, 1995

Michael Wacks, FBI Special Agent, overheard Vannatter
conversation with Fiato brothers   September 20, 1995

Larry Fiato, organized crime informant who met with
Vannatter   September 20, 1995

Craig Fiato, organized crime informant who met with
Vannatter   September 20, 1995